Freedom Within
The Kingdom of God

Diane M. Neumann

Freedom Within The Kingdom of God

Embrace Your God-given Purpose

*A*dvantage
BOOKS

Diane M. Neumann

Published by: ADVANTAGE BOOKS™
                  Longwood, Florida, USA
                  www.advbookstore.com

Library of Congress Catalog Number: 2025931817

Name: Neumann, Diane M., Author
Title: Freedom Within The Kingdom by Diane M. Neumann
                  Advantage Books, 2024
Identifiers: ISBN: Paperback: 9781597558310
                         eBook: 9781597558389
Subjects: RELIGION: Christian Life – Inspirational

First Printing: February 2025
25 26 27 28 29 30 31 32   10 9 8 7 6 5 4 3 2 1

Table of Contents

Diane M. Neumann

1

The Kingdom of God

John the Baptist declared the Kingdom of God is at hand (Matthew 3:2). The Hebrew word for "at hand" is a verb, "enzgizo". It is the action of moving towards a goal. God is announcing to his people, his Kingdom is close and moving towards the unity of the Heavenly Realm with the Earthly Realm in a greater alignment. This is what is prayed in the Lord's Prayer, when stating, "Thy Kingdom Come, thy will be done on earth as it is in Heaven" (Matthew 6:10). God, the Creator, intends a greater unity between his Heavenly Realm and the Earthly Realm. At the end of the Bible, in Revelation, a description of the completion of this unity is given (Revelation 21:1 -2). As in all things God has created in our Cosmos there is a principle of planting, growing and harvesting (Genesis 8:22). It is a principle for life within the spiritual realm. God develops life through regulated seasons and patterns. In the Cosmos God created, he used the same principle. We live in a Cosmos whose blueprint for existence is found in the spiritual realm. The existence of our Cosmos is dependent on alignment with the source of life in the Heavenly Realms. What we know in our physical seen world is this reflection of what is known in the unseen spiritual realm (Hebrews 11:3).

John the Baptist was a prophet of God. He was led by the Holy Spirit to declare the changing of a season or eon of time within the seen world. God determined his plans for the uniting of the Heavenly Realms and the Cosmos Realm had reached a pre-determined mark. So as his word states, he told his prophet to announce it and prepare the people of faith for the next step (Amos 3:7). John was announcing a shift in seasons or a fulfillment of time. John as a prophet is declaring an eon is ending as marked in Heavenly Courts. He is also announcing a new season, with new requirements for his people to stay under the authority of God. As recorded in Isaiah 46:9 - 10

> *⁹Remember the former things of old, For I am God, and there is no other; I am God, and there is none like Me, ¹⁰declaring the end from the beginning, and from ancient times things that are not yet done, Saying, 'My counsel shall stand, And I will do all My pleasure,*

John declared to the people of God an action required to align with this new season. John is telling the people to repent. Strong's number G3340 interprets the Hebrew word, repent, "metanoeo", as to turn away. John is calling them to turn from old patterns of behavior that offend God and accept a new mindset. To end old behaviors a new understanding is required to overtake their former thinking. Our God is a relational God. He created humanity to be his family. When he announces a shift, he tells his people what is expected of them to enter the shift within a positive relationship with God. So those people who feared and honor God completed the actions as recorded in Matthew 3:5 – 6

> *⁵Then Jerusalem, all Judea, and all the region around the Jordan went out to him ⁶and were baptized by him in the Jordan, confessing their sins.*

A cleansing of one's soul body was accomplished by those who responded. It was a preparation to make room in their souls for God's presence in a new way.

Even after the execution of John, the declaration of the shift in the seasons of God was continued. Jesus immediately took up the call of John as recorded in Mark 1:14 – 15

> *¹⁴Now after John was put in prison, Jesus came to Galilee, preaching the gospel of the kingdom of God, ¹⁵and saying, "The time is fulfilled, and the kingdom of God is at hand. Repent, and believe in the gospel."*

Jesus reinforces John's words declaring the ending of a season in God's Kingdom in Heavenly Realms. Jesus invokes the power and authority as a son of man, given to all humanity during creation of our Cosmos. We are made in the likeness of our God and share his attributes (Gensis 1:27). As God speaks in Heavenly Realms, he creates. When we speak under the authority and will of God, we can bring into our realm what already exists in Heavenly Realms. Thus, the Lord's Prayer states: "as it is in heaven". When we align our will to the will of God and declare the truths that exists in Heavenly Realms in this Cosmos, we are pulling that eternal living truth into our lives (Mark 11:23 – 24). It is bringing the Kingdom God into our regions as Jesus taught us to pray. Jesus was enacting the authority given to us as described in Job 22:28

> *You will also declare a thing, and it will be established for you; So, light will shine on your ways.*

This light is further defined in John chapter one. The light and truth that is in Heavenly Realms breaks through into our Cosmos overcoming all darkness that is against God's will (John 1:5). When Jesus is described in the Gospel of John, he is called the light of God. As stated in John 1:3 – 5

> *³All things were made through Him, and without Him nothing was made that was made. ⁴In Him was life, and the life was the light of men. ⁵And the light shines in the darkness, and the darkness did not comprehend it.*

When Jesus was announcing the Kingdom of God was at hand, he was calling to the faithful remnant of Israel to trust God and his ways. Those who placed their faith in God above what they were seeing in the natural world were being called to participate in the new era. He continued the prophetic call of John to maintain what John had begun. Jesus again stated the action needed was to let go of old understanding and turn into the new understanding God was declaring from the Heavenly Realms. He was reminding the faithful the truth of proverbs 3: 5 - 6

⁵Trust in the LORD with all your heart and lean not on your own understanding; ⁶In all your ways acknowledge Him, And He shall direct your paths.

Jesus adds the direction of the new pathway to his statements. Not only are they to let go of the past understanding but also embrace the new known as the Gospel. The Hebrew word of "euangelion" translates to gospel. Strong's number for it is G2098. As with all Hebrew words there are layers of understanding buried in it. The Hebrew word contains a promised future of a Kingdom Age where the Kingdom of God is united in peace with the Cosmos. "Gospel" also is the message and hope of good tidings from God of his will overcoming all darkness. Another nuance of "Gospel" is a manifestation of all the goodness of the Heavenly Kingdom within the Cosmos. Through faith and by their actions, the remnant believers in Israel are demonstrating a trust in God's ways over their own. It is the hope and expectation that God is enacting this process now in their lives. This is to be their response to the declaration Jesus is making. At this point Jesus is not declaring how this will happen only telling them to believe and trust God is doing a new thing.

God knew the end he was seeking and developed the methods on how to reach this end. He determined the seasons and marked them with events that would take place. As noted in Isaiah 14:24

> *The LORD of hosts has sworn, saying, "Surely, as I have thought, so it shall come to pass, and as I have purposed, so it shall stand."*

This creation, humanity, would be like no other. He declared they would be his inheritance. Part of God's original plan for this new creation, was Jesus Christ would enter this created world in the form of a human. Before the foundation of the world was laid (1 Peter1:20) Jesus Christ, a member of the Godhead, agreed to the process of not only making himself less and entering the world but also dying as a sacrifice to reconcile everything in heaven and earth to the original pattern and plan of our triune God (Colossians 1:20). As stated later in Ephesians, (Ephesians 1:9 -11) this plan was made a mystery, to be fulfilled in the fullness of time determined by God.

Jesus who was to complete this assignment was announcing to the faithful people of God to prepare their souls for these events. In trust and in faith they were to expect a mighty move of God. They were to be willing to grow their faith in a new understanding of God's truth. This move of God was to usher in a new eon, within the Cosmos. As God's word states in his Bible, God will achieve greater unity of the Heavenly Kingdom and the Kingdom of the Cosmos as he plans. The plan and the actions to carry it out are still moving forward. God has been speaking to his prophets again telling them how to prepare his believers for this next move to manifest the Kingdom of God on earth as it is in heaven. Through the action of the Holy Spirit, God is revealing a deeper understanding of his word to those who will seek him with all their hearts. Now is the time to obey Jesus' direction to first seek the Kingdom of God and His Righteousness.

Battle within the Cosmos

Basic to understanding God's ways is to know the source of the resistance to God's plans. It is obvious to those living in our Cosmos we lack peace. Jesus Christ promised a peace beyond what the world gives (John 14:27). This peace is found in aligning with the original living spiritual structure and blueprint of creation. Anything outside of this blueprint creates chaos and disruption. Since we live in a Cosmos that has violence, chaos and destruction, something else must be functioning in our Cosmos that is not sanctioned under God's authority. This something is spiritual in nature.

Before the creation of humanity, there was a rebellion in the Heavenly Realms. A being known as the Son of the Morning Star or Lucifer chose to act outside of the will of God. In disobedience he used his anointing and gifts to create for himself an alternative plan for the newly created Cosmos. Rebellion and a plan to develop an alternative authority within the Cosmos was fostered in this disobedience. As recorded in Isaiah 14:12 - 14

> *12How you are fallen from heaven, O Lucifer, son of the morning! How you are cut down to the ground, you who weakened the nations! 13For you have said in your heart:*

'I will ascend into heaven, I will exalt my throne above the stars of God; I will also sit on the mount of the congregation on the farthest sides of the north; [14]I will ascend above the heights of the clouds, I will be like the Most High.'

Isaiah is recording the motive of the rebellion. A desire for greatness is bred in Lucifer's heart. He is choosing to exalt himself, thus valuing pride in self above honoring and serving the Creator. Like all creatures in Heavenly Realms Lucifer was created by our triune God. Lucifer's actions generate a dissonance to the harmony and balance in the Heavenly Realms. God delineates who he created Lucifer to be and what happened in Lucifer's heart. As recorded in Ezekiel 28:14, 17

[14]You were the anointed cherub who covers; I established you; You were on the holy mountain of God; You walked back and forth in the midst of fiery stones. [15]You were perfect in your ways from the day you were created, till iniquity was found in you.

[17]Your heart was lifted up because of your beauty; You corrupted your wisdom for the sake of your splendor; I cast you to the ground, I laid you before kings, that they might gaze at you.

God chose to remove Lucifer from Heavenly Realms. God allowed this rejected being to be seen and known by his new creation humanity. Heart attitudes in God's created beings effect their obedience to their created purposes. These attitudes affect actions and have consequences. Those who choose to serve God in obedience align with God's will. They maintain their position in the overall plan God has for his Cosmos. Order, harmony and peace reign where each created being serves in their assigned positions. All creation benefits from each one fulfilling their role and purpose. This is why God calls his people to choose life and align with his will (Deuteronomy 30:19).

The method of the removal of Lucifer from Heavenly Realms is recorded in another section of the Bible. This event in heaven is described in spiritual reality in Revelations. It is recorded in Revelations to explain the origin of the dragon. As recorded in Revelations 12:7 – 9

> *[7]And war broke out in heaven: Michael and his angels fought with the dragon; and the dragon and his angels fought, [8]but they did not prevail, nor was a place found for them in heaven any longer. [9]So the great dragon was cast out, that serpent of old, called the Devil and Satan, who deceives the whole world; he was cast to the earth, and his angels were cast out with him.*

The results of Lucifer being cast out of heaven are his presence on earth and his works as a deceiver in our Cosmos. This action is confirmed in 2 Peter 2:4.

The result of the great dragon, or Satan being in the Cosmos is explained in 2 Corinthians 4:3 - 4

> *[3]But even if our gospel is veiled, it is veiled to those who are perishing, [4]whose minds the god of this age has blinded, who do not believe, lest the light of the gospel of the glory of Christ, who is the image of God, should shine on them.*

The intent of the fallen being Lucifer, known also as the great dragon, or Satan or the devil is to deceive humanity. It is to prevent them from fulfilling the plans and purpose of God for his Cosmos. It is to cover with deception and darkness the truth within the light of God. Satan's purpose is still to create and alternative world in the Cosmos so he may rise and be like God. He seeks the position God created humanity to hold in the Cosmos (Gensis 1:26).

Satan's actions began in the Garden of Eden with twisting God's words and building doubt in the heart of people (Genesis 3:1). The result was a prophesy God released as a judgment on the implementation and actions of all who participated in the eating of the fruit of the Tree of Knowledge of Good and Evil (Genesis 3:14 – 19). Satan desired humanity to surrender our authority to him. He also needed our souls to carry the knowledge of evil so we could be tempted like him. Satan's heart was corrupted by pride, and desires for power and authority. Satan is a being of spirit and lacks a physical body. He needed a way to act within a physical body with the soul body connected to it to build his alternative world. Corrupting the soul heart of humanity accomplished all of these purposes. Now Satan had an avenue to change the plans of God for his Cosmos to become the plans of Satan.

God's plans continued to move forward throughout the history of the Cosmos. Jesus Christ came and reconciled everything in heaven and earth. All that was out of the original order and harmony with God's will and His Heavenly Realm was restored. As recorded in Colossians 1:19 – 22

> *[19]For it pleased the Father that in Him all the fullness should dwell, [20]and by Him to reconcile all things to Himself, by Him, whether things on earth or things in heaven, having made peace through the blood of His cross. [21]And you, who once were alienated and enemies in your mind by wicked works, yet now He has reconciled [22]in the body of His flesh through death, to present you holy, and blameless, and above reproach in His sight—*

By entering in faith, the Covenant of Blood of Jesus Christ, through the grace of God, we have the benefits of what Jesus Christ accomplished (Ephesians 2:7 -8). Unfortunately, the battle in our Cosmos does not end here. Though we may accept the total victory of Jesus Christ, we also can choose to reject it. When we reject it, we are still subject to the Tree of Knowledge of Good and Evil and Satan's temptations.

Now on this side of the cross of Jesus, followers of Jesus Christ are called to enforce the victory of Jesus. We use the spiritual weapons God has given us to take back spiritual territory Satan claims. The Word of God is one of the powerful spiritual weapons. The Word includes what is recorded in the Bible and also what is released through prophesy. The Holy Spirit guides believers in all truth as Jesus stated he would (John 14:16 -17 & John16:7 – 11). When we work in tandem with the Word and the Holy Spirit, they guide us and shows us the methods of Satan and how to overcome them.

Daniel was told of the method Satan uses to accomplish his goal against the followers of Jesus Christ. In Daniel 7:25 (KJV)

> *He shall speak pompous words against the Most High, Shall wear out the saints of the Most High, And shall intend to change times and law. Then the saints shall be given into his hand for a time and times and half a time.*

The enemy's strategy is the same one he used in the Garden. Now he is questioning whether we trust our covenant with God. Do we stand in faith, trusting God will provide and protect or can Satan get us to lean into our own strength? He attacks by asking if God did accomplish what we believe. If he can sow doubt, he can force each believer back into the Tree of Knowledge of Good and Evil. Satan can delude us into thinking we have to fight at the soul level the battle that Jesus Christ as already won. Trapped in the fight within our soul, we chip away at our trust in God and gradually become double minded. So, we are attacked with things in this world to wear us out. If he can break our trust in God, then our faith weakens. It is a slow wearing down emotionally, physically and mentally.

Our answer is to rise up in faith and enter the Heavenly Kingdom of God. We have access through the Blood Covenant of Jesus Christ. Those who have entered the Covenant of the Blood of Jesus with God are protected by the covenant. We enter this covenant by the grace of God as a gift from God. When we follow the instructions given to us by Jesus Christ, we become more than conquerors and defeat all the plans and strategies of Satan (Romans 8:37). It is an act of living faith and trust that holds God's people in this covenant.

In recent world history we, the people of God have been experiencing Satan's works as Daniel described them. This book addresses ways to be the overcomers under the authority Jesus gave us as we stand in faith and trust. There is a way out of the fruit of the Knowledge of the Tree of Good and Evil. Now is the time to move into this new era and embrace the truth of our pray:

Thy will be done, Thy Kingdom Come, God In earth as it is in your Heavenly Kingdom.

2

The Cosmos

Genesis 1:1 In the beginning God created the heavens and the earth.

Our triune God designated patterns, cycles, frequencies, and movement when He created the heavens and the earth. Order, form, and energy were imposed through the will of our God. We, the believers in Jesus Christ as our Lord, stand in faith, as stated in Hebrews 11:3

> *By faith we understand that the worlds were framed by the word of God, so that the things which are seen were not made of things which are visible.*

Out of the mouth of God, came pronouncements, full of spirit, that vibrated from where God exists, in the unseen Heavenly Realms, into what we know as our visible world. The voice of God, in the eternal Heavenly Realms broke forth and created the seen world. Thus, the seen world is always subject to the eternal Heavenly Realms. The source or blueprint has authority over what it produced. By the term, visible world, we mean anything known through our senses. This includes what is learned and observed through human created technology. Technology includes instruments that allow us to see inside the human body, the microscopic world, the depths of the earth or the expanse of cosmos. It also includes instruments that enhance all our senses from simple eyeglasses to clothing that enhances a sense of touch. We believe behind what is known in this visible world, there is a spirit world called Heavenly Realms. This world of spirit is learned and known by our spirit bodies (1 Corinthians 2:10 – 13). The eternal Heavenly Realms are the source of all creation. It is through faith humanity functions in the invisible world, the Heavenly Realms. As stated in Hebrews 11: 1

Now faith is the substance of things hoped for, the evidence of things not seen.

To enter and know within this spiritual Heavenly Realms, humanity seeks not with known senses in our physical bodies but rather by applying faith within a spiritual body created by our God.

In the spiritual account of creation, found in Genesis, we learn humanity is a three-fold being. As recorded in Genesis 1:26 - 27, God stated:

> ²⁶*Then God said, "Let Us make man in Our image, according to Our likeness; let them have dominion over the fish of the sea, over the birds of the air, and over the cattle, over all the earth and over every creeping thing that creeps on the earth." ²⁷So God created man in His own image; in the image of God, He created him; male and female He created them.*

The Elohim, the Jewish word for God, in this passage is the plural form. Being created in the image of God means having a three-fold being as Elohim (God) does. Later in the Bible the nature of the three-fold being of God is explained.

The Bible states Jesus Christ is the son of God, sharing in his power and authority. Jesus Christ is recognized a member of the Elohim as the passages in Hebrews 1: 1 – 3 explains.

> ¹*God, who at various times and in various ways spoke in time past to the fathers by the prophets, ²has in these last days spoken to us by His Son, whom He has appointed heir of all things, through whom also He made the worlds; ³who being the brightness of His glory and the express image of His person, and upholding all things by the word of His power, when He had by Himself purged our sins, sat down at the right hand of the Majesty on high,*

In this passage two of the beings of Elohim, God, that is mentioned in the creation story in Genesis are explained. Father God is known through his relationship with his son, Jesus Christ. When Jesus Christ completed his mission on the earth, he returned to his place in our unseen Heavenly Realms. Jesus Christ is the right hand of God. Jesus Christ function is explained in Colossians 1:15 - 17

[15]He is the image of the invisible God, the firstborn over all creation. [16]For by Him all things were created that are in heaven and that are on earth, visible and invisible, whether thrones or dominions or principalities or powers. All things were created through Him and for Him. [17]And He is before all things, and in Him all things exist.

The third being of the Elohim is described by Jesus to his disciples. At the last supper, Jesus tells his disciples about events that are to occur. Jesus explains he will be leaving and one of God will come to take his place. In John 16:13 - 15, Jesus states:

[13]"However, when He, the Spirit of truth, has come, He will guide you into all truth; for He will not speak on His own authority, but whatever He hears He will speak; and He will tell you things to come. [14]He will glorify Me, for He will take of what is Mine and declare it to you. [15]All things that the Father has are Mine. Therefore, I said that He will take of mine and declare it to you."

The connection between Father God, Jesus Christ and Spirit of Truth is described. Followers of Jesus Christ also call the Spirit of Truth the Holy Spirit. This is the same spirit mentioned in Genesis that participated in creation. Gensis 1:2b

The earth was without form, and void; and darkness was on the face of the deep. And the Spirit of God was hovering over the face of the waters.

These three beings in God are the Elohim. Together they created the heavens and earth. They chose to create humanity in their image and likeness possessing three bodies which have separate functions yet are united in one.

Just as the Godhead has a spirit, so humanity has a spirit body. The other two are known as physical body and soul body. The physical body contains the senses we are most familiar with and interprets the physical cosmos. The spirit body has an affinity for the Heavenly Realms. It possesses sense organs like the physical body and interprets within the Heavenly Realms. It is through faith that this spirit body is activated and learns how to operate in these Heavenly Realms.

Patterns within the Heavens

According to Genesis, God as Elohim, entered a place called earth which was without form (see Genesis 1:2). The Hebrew word for this substance, earth, is "To-Huw". It conveys the sense of chaos, confusion and without form. Darkness rested upon a deep, which had a form like the waters. The Hebrew word for water in this passage is "Mayim". This picture word represents a combination of filth, semen, and/or urine. The Spirit of God brooded on this dark, wet, void. A void indicates an absence. What was absent? The Spirit of God which creates and maintains life as we know it was absent. Something happened to what God produced to render what was created in love, righteousness, and truth into chaos and void. At the beginning of Genesis, we are seeing God's solution being applied to return what was defiled to the purpose and plans of God. The void contained what we know as death or spiritual corruption. For anything without spirit of God lacks life. It is outside of the created source and disintegrates.

As The spirit of God brooded over this death-like, watery, formless substance, God spoke Light. The function of the light is explained in the book of John chapter one. John introduces Jesus Christ in context to his being the eternal Word, during the process of creation. John 1: 4 – 5

> *⁴In Him was life, and the life was the light of men. ⁵And the light shines in the darkness, and the darkness did not comprehend it.*

When God spoke light into the void, God released life. As noted in Gensis 1:4, God divided the light from the dark. When this is read with only a physical understanding (worldly viewpoint) we read about the physical manifestation of light and darkness. In doing so we limit the truth of all that light is. This spoken light as John noted gives spiritual life. God spoken word is always a vibration that is eternal and spiritually alive. Remember the original source of the word is in Heavenly Realms which have greater authority and power over what is being created in the physical world. God divided this living spirit filled light from darkness. A barrier was created between the elements within the void. One side was fostering corruption and the other side living spiritual light.

John also reveals another spiritual truth about spiritual light. The darkness cannot overcome it. Spiritual living light always will bring forth all the attributes of life as God intends. It will overcome death and chaos as depicted in the void. For our Creator God calls life-light out of darkness-death and created an eternal spiritual pattern. This pattern becomes a living truth in Heavenly Realms. His living truth within the Kingdom of God is that the living eternal spiritual light brings life out of death. Humanity calls this rule resurrection. All of this void substance now is permeated with a spiritual truth of resurrection power of light which overcomes all darkness. Thus, everything created from this now permeated substance carries the possibility of resurrection power over chaos, corruption and death.

God creates his first memorial for humanity in his next act of creation. In this next act of creation of heavens and earth, God gave a pattern to allow humanity to wonder and question. The balanced cycle of darkness and then light, we call night and day is this memorial. Within the new Cosmos, God bound light and darkness into a cycle. The Spiritual properties within Heavenly Realms were not bound. The recorded truth that all of creation has the possibility of resurrection within it is still a spiritual truth alive within the Heavenly realms and available in the Cosmos. This night/day cycle in the physical world would be a repetitive signpost of a hidden mystery within the physical world that reflects a spiritual truth of resurrection. Genesis 1:5 states

God called the light Day, and the darkness He called Night. So, the evening and the morning were the first day.

Humanity would participate in a rhythm. Each day begins with darkness and light is brought forth. It is a daily reminder of the first act of God bringing life out of death. It is a daily reminder that the spiritual light overcomes the spiritual darkness. It holds the promise of resurrection power within all that has been created in the Cosmos. What is seen in the physical is a reminder of a spiritual truth. As noted in Romans 1:20

> *For since the creation of the world His invisible attributes are clearly seen, being understood by the things that are made, even His eternal power and Godhead, so that they are without excuse,*

What is seen in the physical world is intended to bring questions to human minds. We are to search for spiritual meaning in the patterns operating in this cosmos. The questions and wonder are not to be limited by our senses which function in the physical body. Human culture generally agrees there are greater realities, like moral laws, love, and honesty. It is accepted these are not just results of the physical body, but of another source. Humanity speaks of choosing a greater good when examining these realities. An unseen world is acknowledged in these understandings. We are to be awake in our spiritual bodies and seek spiritual truth. This is accomplished by faith.

Faith is a substance in the spiritual world (Hebrews 11:1). Faith opens humanity's spiritual organs to know and function in the Heavenly Realms. Only in faith can we know the source of life, and how life is maintained. In the physical world we can trace the results of life, searching for the footprints left in the visible world by the Heavenly Realms. In essence we are chasing after truth. Paul described this in 1 Corinthians 13:12

> *For now, we see in a mirror, dimly, but then face to face. Now I know in part, but then I shall know just as I also am known.*

When God spoke this cosmos into being, his thoughts and heart desires became our physical reality. He created us in his image and likeness, so we have the attributes to follow these footprints into the spiritual source. Notice Paul connects how we only know it part while functioning in our physical bodies. Even what we are able to sense through our spiritual bodies is only a partial understanding. We are like small children learning to operate in their physical bodies as we grow into our spiritual bodies. Later, when we are face to face with God, we will know as we are known by God. Our greater understanding is dependent on development of our spiritual bodies as we increase our reliance on God.

After creating life giving light, God worked with the waters. On the second day, it is recorded in Genesis 1:6

> *Then God said, "Let there be a firmament in the midst of the waters, and let it divide the waters from the waters."*

First, spiritual death-darkness was separated from spiritual life-giving light. Now a division is created in the midst or middle of the waters. These are the same waters that were brooded over to bring life back into chaos. Within the life-filled waters, a division of a spiritual kind was created. Half of this water is to become part of the earth. Firmament in Hebrew language is *"rāqîa '"*. It *is described as a flat surface to support. God created a dividing place. It is a spiritual barrier. True to the Kingdom of God principles for creation, what is created in the spiritual has a manifestation in the physical. In verse eight it states: Genesis1:6b*

> *And God called the firmament Heaven. So, the evening and the morning were the second day.*

In the physical truth it is a ceiling of air that envelops the earth. The edge of the ceiling, or ozone layer is the physical beginning of the firmament of heavens. Both parts of the original void now are separated, the light and the waters. This firmament was left as this barrier as God called it good and the end of the second day finished its cycle.

The third day is dedicated to structuring the earth below the firmament. The next day, the fourth day is filled with completing the firmament. As stated in Genesis 1:14

> *Then God said, "Let there be lights in the firmament of the heavens to divide the day from the night; and let them be for signs and seasons, and for days and years."*

God is imposing an order on his creation that reflects the order in the Kingdom of God in Heavenly Realms. Though previously, day and night have been created, now multiple rhythm cycles are added. God's voice that creates has a living frequency to it. His words always keep producing to accomplish his complete goal (Isaiah 55: 8 – 11). The seasons add a rhythm which brings an order and balance to the frequency. It is here God adds the limiting sequence to his creation that we know as time. Time is less than eternity in power and authority. Time is birthed from the Heavenly Realms through the nature of God. It is a limitation God imposes on the seen physical world. By creating the repetitive seasons, cycles are now established within time. Minor cycles are encompassed in the larger cycles, such as seasons which are held within years. The spiritual truth hidden within time reflects how God moves in Heavenly Realms. Cycles and order in Heavenly Realms bring order and symmetry. The frequencies and vibrations form patterns in Heavenly Realms that maintain the established order. These are cyclical.

A spiritual truth of heavenly realms is imposed now on the Cosmos. As recorded in Ecclesiastes 3:1-2

> *To everything there is a season, A time for every purpose under heaven: ²A time to be born, and a time to die; A time to plant, and a time to pluck what is planted.*

Time has a purpose determined in Heavenly Realm where greater authority exists. The order has a season of birthing and growing to maturity. Then time is given to plant the seeds or fruit of the maturity process. This will yield a harvest, that will be gathered. In another section the Bible explains the same spiritual truth this way. As recorded in Genesis 8:22

> *While the earth remains, Seedtime and harvest, Cold and heat, Winter and summer, and day and night Shall not cease."*

All the substances of the created Cosmos are subjugated to this Heavenly Realm truth. The quality of life for beings within the cosmos will depend on submitting to this Heavenly Realm truth.

This system of seasons and cycles is held in check by the next created elements within the firmament. A larger cycle is imposed over the balance of seasons, day/night. As explained in Genesis 1: 16 – 18

> [16]*Then God made two great lights: the greater light to rule the day, and the lesser light to rule the night. He made the stars also.* [17]*God set them in the firmament of the heavens to give light on the earth,* [18]*and to rule over the day and over the night, and to divide the light from the darkness. And God saw that it was good.*

Light holds the spiritual element of life. The sun is filled with the spiritual source of life. The moon reflects this source of spiritual life. Another spiritual truth is held in the relationship between the sun and moon. Just as God pours his love into his creation, the creation is to reflect back the love to the Creator. The sun and moon embody this spiritual truth. This interdependent relationship has a pattern that affects all around it. As they pour through the firmament into the canopy of the physical earth, they provide spiritual nourishment as well as allowing life to grow in the physical world. The unseen spiritual energy invades and monitors the physical world. The physical world is dependent on this nourishment balance to maintain life. These are now integrated with a greater rhythm and frequency within the earth.

The stars also have cycles and rhythms. These substances in the firmament have longer frequency and cycles. The cycles within cycles and the necessity for sunlight for growth were given to humanity to wonder what maintains their balance, order and life. All heavenly bodies were to be a second memorial for humanity to wonder and seek their creator.

The moon was to hold an additional mystery. To natural eyes, the moon appears to grow and shrink or what humanity calls waxes and wanes. This has a regular night/day component of twenty-eight days. Humanity uses it for measuring time and defining order. God uses it to show a mystery. The Bible speaks of the fulness of time. Galatians 4:4 - 5 states

> *⁴But when the fullness of the time had come, God sent forth His Son, born of a woman, born under the law, ⁵to redeem those who were under the law, that we might receive the adoption as sons.*

An event was determined to happen based on the fullness of time. When other events had occurred, God judged the earth was ripe for this coming of Jesus Christ. "Fullness of time" is also used In Ephesians 1:9 – 10

> *⁹having made known to us the mystery of His will, according to His good pleasure which He purposed in Himself, ¹⁰that in the dispensation of the fullness of the times He might gather together in one all things in Christ, both which are in heaven, and which are on earth— in Him.*

"Dispensation" is a term meaning management. By the will of God, our creator, judges when events have been completed to meet his plans. Then, it is the fullness of time and God moves to the next stage. The two events of the birth of Jesus then the gathering of his people have steps that are described in scripture that are to occur in a God determined order.

The cycles of the moon from dark to fullness and then to dark are rhythms in a synchronized predictable time frame. God intended for people to seek him through these signs and wonder what it might mean about the nature of God and his plans. As we reflect on the effects of waxing and waning of the moon, we are to wonder as we examine how this affects our earth. The fulness of the moon, and the rhythm that creates it is a symbol for God's plans to have a sequence, and rhythm that is dependent on the greater source of light-life, the sun. We, his creation, are dependent on the greater source, Heavenly Realms for our source. As stated in the Bible, we live and move and have our being in God (Acts17:28). We are to align to the leading of the light and move as it does to receive the benefits of the light-life of God.

God gives multiple layers of meaning and revelation in his creation. Creation is imbued with eternal spiritual truth. When humanity studies the moon and the relationship to the earth, the waters of the oceans are noticed to match the cycle of the moon and the moon's relationship to the sun. The heavenly bodies movement affects the oceans' movements. Tides are predictable when the heavens are considered. The inter-relationship of heaven and earth is realized. When humanity takes advantage of this wisdom, dependence on heavenly body rhythm enhances industry based on oceans. A sign in the earthly realm reflects a Kingdom of God principle. This is the principle of waves and dependency. When we seek God through surrendering to Jesus Christ as Lord, we become dependent on a greater outside force. Our dependency is found in the Heavenly Realms. When we depend on this greater wisdom, we can move in waves of revelations of our God. Our industry is more productive for we are now moving in unity with God's ways and plans. We are more fruitful thus fulfilling are original created mandate as Sons of God (Genesis1:28).

Patterns within the Earth

God impregnated the earth with seed bearing life. As noted in Genesis 1:11 – 12

> *[11]Then God said, "Let the earth bring forth grass, the herb that yields seed, and the fruit tree that yields fruit according to its kind, whose seed is in itself, on the earth"; and it was so. [12]And the earth brought forth grass, the herb that yields seed according to its kind, and the tree that yields fruit, whose seed is in itself according to its kind. And God saw that it was good.*

God gave the power to the earth to bring forth the purpose that is in each seed. The earth, like all created substances, carries the spiritual truth of resurrection power. God is now declaring that spiritual truth to manifest. The spiritual living force in the land is called to activate what is held within the seed. God's pattern was that the seed of all living things would carry the definition of self, and its purpose according to its kind. The interaction of the resurrection power in the earth and the purpose and identity within the seed would activate growth held within the seed. The Hebrew word for earth is a feminine noun, "eres", giving it the quality of a womb to nurture what is in the seed to be released. "Zera" is the Hebrew word for seed. It is a masculine noun. A spiritual pattern of the dependency of two elements to release life from a seed is established.

We see evidence of this in the physical world. Notice on rocky areas how small tress will grow in cracks in rocks. See how grass and weeds will sprout in cracks in cement. After forest fires, seeds will immediately start to grow where all has been destroyed. It is the spiritual nature of the earth that is calling forth the life in the seeds to be released in these situations. Contaminated soil and corrupted soil are hindered from meeting the spiritual truth. If enough corruption in layered into the soil, it takes on the form of the original substance that the Elohim resurrected. By the actions of applying God's principles to the soil it can be re-vitalized to again serve its spiritual purpose.

In God's blueprint for life on earth, everything that has life has a "seed". The DNA of all living entities carries the truth of what the entity will be. This is God's statement "according to its kind". The fruit that produces the seed is not limited to vegetation. Propagation of a species depends on the original source to copy the DNA and unite with another strand of DNA to form a "seed". As defined by God, "whose seed is in itself". Whether it is a one cell organism or a large multi-cellular organism, each carries the seed within it during the cycle of reproduction. The reproductive cycles in living entities are as varied as are the species. The spiritual truth that governs them is recorded in Heavenly Realms. Again, God uses cycles to highlight life dependency on a moving process. It reflects the spiritual truth of the laws in Heavenly Realms.

On the fifth day of creation, God applies the same principle of seed/reproduction to the animals he placed in the waters of earth and the air above the earth. A variety of shapes, material and habits were developed by

God. He filled these places with life carrying creatures. Humanity is drawn to them to wonder. The similarities and differences were to draw humans into appreciating the limitless possibilities to God's handiwork. Anomalies like creatures with wings who do not fly, or hummingbirds who do with such a high rate of movement they have to eat all the time are wonders and signs of God's creative mind. Science is still trying to determine what within the physical body of geese triggers birds to fly south for winter. Just as the vastness of the night sky should bring amazement, so should the variety of creatures also cause humble appreciation for our God's wisdom.

God Creates Humanity

God creatively formed a triune being, humanity to possess the qualities and abilities of himself (Genesis 1: 26). Since God is three in one, so shall humanity possess three interdependent bodies. One of the three bodies of humanity was created out of the substance of the cosmos, the dirt. As stated in Genesis 2:7

> *And the LORD God formed man of the dust of the ground and breathed into his nostrils the breath of life; and man became a living being.*

The spiritual properties God imbued into the dirt were retained in the physical body of humanity. This body is dependent on these spiritual laws embedded into our Cosmos to exist. All that is true for the earth, such as limited by time and held with cycles are also true of this physical body. The spiritual laws of reproduction written in Heavenly Realms for living creatures in our Cosmos also apply to the physical body.

Because God spoke his intent and purpose for humanity, his words contain unique spiritual essences (Genesis 1:26 – 27). In Heavenly Realms this spoken word is alive and keeps producing its intended goal (Isaish 55:11). In other words, Adam's spirit was spoken into existence when God released his declaration in heavenly Realms (Genesis1:26). The vibrations of the words of God weave a pattern into the Heavenly Realms that create a unity of substance and love (Heavenly energy). This is the eternal spiritual substance of humanity we call our spirit bodies. These spiritual substances are the spiritual or second body of humanity. The spiritual body is eternal. The blending of the earthly spiritual essence and the new spiritual essence of humanity in the Cosmos are balanced through a third body. We call this third body our soul body. The third body of humanity came from the breath of God, poured into Adam through his nostrils. Essentially God exhaled and Adam inhaled God's breath. The air Adam breathed entered into his lungs and then his bloodstream. A unity of God's presence in his breath with his creation brings life through the carrier, the blood of Adam. This is why the Bible states the life is in the blood (Lev.17:11). Adam became a living soul (1 Corinthians 15:45). While living in our cosmos in all three bodies, blood is essential for maintaining life in the physical body. The blood now is the mediator between the spirit body of humanity and the physical body of humanity in the cosmos God created. This unity in the blood is sacred to God.

3

Heavenly Realm Substances

There is a mutual sharing, weaving, and interdependence between God the Father, God Jesus Christ, and God, Holy Spirit as they interact with each other in Heavenly Realms. We, his creation, recognize this as sound, harmony, rhythm, light, movement, and color. Each manifestation has a vibration, or variation within these forms and is also a unique expression. Love is the energy of Heaven. It is the living, moving, force behind all creation. It transforms, morphs, and moves. It vibrates with a sound or voice we identify as music. It intertwines leaving pathways of color and light. This pathway is the substance marking what has been created with sound vibrations. The love is still alive and moving in what we recognize, transforming and changing, yet also holding its essence of original sound. It moves like quantum physics, changing from energy to substance to energy in the pathway just constructed. In the now moment, it is both substance and energy. This pathway is transmutated into a form we identify as righteousness. The substance of the pathway, righteousness, becomes the building blocks of the cosmos as we know it. Righteousness interconnects as it is maintained through the energy of love. It is dynamic. As God examines these structures, he makes decisions to modify or fix the righteousness as elements in eternity. What he deems "good" is chosen to be fixed in that form. This unity of righteousness and love becomes living truth defining all we can comprehend (Psalm 119:142). Simply put God shared love moves to build and forms righteousness. When God deems this unity "good" it becomes all living eternal truth.

In intimate fellowship with God, we seek who he is. We have developed a relationship with our God and can, as the Bible states, "know the voice of God" (John 10:27). We enter into heavenly realms through the doorway that is Jesus Christ (John 14:6 & John 10:7). In our awakened spiritual bodies, as we search within Heavenly Realms, we find true love and the righteousness that holds our cosmos together. When we function in our spiritual bodies, we learn to let go of what is previously understood, to embrace new revelation. This is the action of faith. As we communicate with God in spirit, we may receive revelation. When new revelation enters our spirit bodies, we trust and obey where this is leading us. Our worship, faith, trust, and love now enter the patterns we sense. We literally behold the Glory of God and also become one with it. As it states in the 2 Corinthians 3:18

> *But we all, with unveiled face, beholding as in a mirror the glory of the Lord, are being transformed into the same image from glory to glory, just as by the Spirit of the Lord.*

Spiritual truth is alive. It is eternal, forming the blueprint for all else that is created in our cosmos (Hebrews11:3). This truth undergirds and supports all life within our cosmos. The combination of the energy of love and the substance of righteousness holds what is created in our cosmos together. Since God is and is also creating and thus changing like quantum, only in moving in love can we truly comprehend God. He is the living energy and the stability of righteousness (Psalm 89:14). The quantum understanding of being form and movement best explains this eternal principle of who God is.

This is why the heavenly Kingdom principle is to worship in spirit and truth. Worship and surrender to God as Lord opens the doorway into Heavenly Realms. We align with what is alive as we surrender ourselves and limited wisdom and knowledge to greater truth. We literally die to self, old ways, and enter seeking God's patterns for the now. Jesus Christ is the truth, the way, and the door into the unseen spiritual realm (John14:6). He goes before us, leading us into all truth. In worship we enter the intertwining of love, as we surrender ourselves as an offering of love and gratitude. As stated in Romans 12:1(NIV)

Therefore, I urge you, brothers and sisters, in view of God's mercy, to offer your bodies as a living sacrifice, holy and pleasing to God—this is your true and proper worship.

We give up, or sacrifice, our perspectives, our definition of self, and offer our bodies for Jesus Christ to unite with in a greater way.

Believers in Jesus understand by grace Jesus lives in us. When we turn our focus by spirit into who lives in us, Jesus Christ, and call out into the spiritual realm, we reach up through our faith to search spirit to spirit for the presence of Jesus Christ. Heavenly Realms operate under the principle of like attracts to like. He who is in us, Jesus Christ leads us into his presence in Heavenly Realms. As we connect in faith and spirit, our love bonds with God's love. Unity of love creates harmony and a symphony within the spiritual realm. God inhabits the praises of His people (Psalm 22:3).

A mystery is that God is changing and forever the same. We can only grasp this when we move in his perfect love in faith and trust. It is a constant letting go of self to enter a greater unity. We sense a completion when we are in the midst of this unity. It is a spiritual memory recognized within our eternal spiritual bodies (Ecclesiastes 3:11). This is what Paul is describing in Ephesians chapter one. As stated in Ephesians 1:4

Just as He chose us in Him before the foundation of the world, that we should be holy and without blame before Him in love,

Before our cosmos was created, God knew us. Where were we before our cosmos existed? We were in Father God. Before we were planted in our mother's wombs we existed in spiritual form in Father God as living spirits (Psalm 139:16). The rest of the Ephesian quote explains our destiny and purpose while in this cosmos. We are to become like God, holy and blameless. Notice it is in love we can accomplish this directive. We cannot accomplish this is our own strength, our own wisdom, or our own righteousness (Romans 3:10 – 12). When we seek God with our whole heart, in love we will find him. This is the love like God's love. Jesus stated in John 15:10

*If you keep My commandments, you will abide in My love, just as I
have kept My Father's commandments and abide in His love.*

Abiding in Father God's love is trusting his love above everything we see
and know in our physical bodies, our own understanding and our learned
experiences. Obedience, trust, and surrender are keys to living within the
commandments of Jesus Christ. These three are all spiritual actions of
sacrificing self to God. They are actions of love as God loves. It is not by our
own works or abilities that we can become holy and blameless. Jesus Christ
accomplished this on the cross. We accept his sacrifice through the grace of
God (Ephesians 2:8). The commandments Jesus mentions are the expression
of the truth of Heavenly Realms written in the fabric of what was created by
God. The pattern Jesus accomplished, becomes a living spiritual truth. In
essence one could call it a law within Heavenly Realms. Remember truth is
the outcome of love and righteousness. They are intertwined. We are to focus
on how we enter this "abiding". It is not the commandments that govern
abiding in Father God as much as it is the surrender, trust, and obedience.
Just as faith is the vehicle to enter heavenly realms so is obedience, trust and
surrender the tool to abide in God's love.

The letters Paul wrote examine the false approach of putting the law or
commandments before seeking God through grace. It is putting our efforts
and actions before we surrender to the greater truth of who Jesus Christ is.
As he summarized in Romans 3:28 - 29

> *[28]A person is not a Jew who is one only outwardly, nor is
> circumcision merely outward and physical. [29]No, a person is a Jew
> who is one inwardly; and circumcision is circumcision of the heart,
> by the Spirit, not by the written code. Such a person's praise is not
> from other people, but from God.*

God always intended for those he created in his likeness, humanity, to
function in their spirits and live out of their hearts. The law and
commandments were given to teach how to accomplish this. It was through
the sense of failing under our own might and strength we would turn to God
(Romans 7:21-24). We were to surrender and sacrifice our ways and ask God

to enter into us to accomplish what we could not do on our own. As Paul further explains in Romans 3:20

> *Therefore no one will be declared righteous in God's sight by the works of the law; rather, through the law we become conscious of our sin.*

Through our own might and efforts, we become a slave to what we hate (Romans 7: 14 -15). Seeking holiness by our own actions is living in the constant fight to do what is right and overcome the temptations which control our thoughts and energy. This is living by the fruits of the Tree of Knowledge of Good and Evil. We judge what is right and good by our experiences and conditions. We interpret commandments and decide guilt or innocence. Much energy is expended in our souls as we try and stop the development of such thoughts into actions. In addition to these soul activities, another action happens within our soul. As we follow the law, claiming righteousness by our own behaviors, this process denies the byproduct of these actions. Other sins are born as we focus on using our own strength to follow the commandments. These byproducts include sins such as pride, arrogance, manipulation of others, as well as burying shame and remorse. We trade the repentance or avoidance of gross sins for less recognizable ones that are still sin. We are still stuck in the Tree of Knowledge of Good and Evil. This is why Jesus stated his commandments was to love as he loved and to love one another (John13:34). In seeking righteousness through love, we are aligning with the very fabric of creation.

The commandments Jesus is telling us to follow, his commandments to love as God loves. God loves by sacrifice. The much-quoted scripture verifies Father God sacrifice. John 3:16

> *For God so loved the world that he gave his one and only Son, that whoever believes in him shall not perish but have eternal life.*

Father God gave his only begotten son. He gave his best in the hope that those who received this gift would choose to accept and leave their own ways and understanding. In surrendering their ways, they enter through Jesus

Christ into a greater relationship with God. All the works of Jesus while on earth are recorded in Heavenly Realms. They have become living spiritual truths. The requirements of the Courts of heaven to break the hold of the Tree of Knowledge of Good and Evil were met by the actions of Jesus (1 Peter 2:24). It is accepted through faith, a spiritual act not an earthly act. Faith is an action accomplished in the soul and spirit bodies. It is the key to entering the eternal Heavenly Realms. This process of surrendering through faith and seeking into the Heavenly Realms functions under spiritual laws and principles. As Father God sacrificed, so are we to sacrifice to come in deeper in relationship with our Creator God. Remember, we are made in their likeness. What God ordains by his actions and approves as "good' becomes truth. These truths are what sustains what God has created. By his actions God made an eternal truth of sacrifice to be a vehicle to enter into the presence of God.

Faith given in love transmutes and becomes a spiritual substance in Heavenly Realms. Jesus Christ sacrificed his own physical body to satisfy the requirements of the law of sin and death in the Heavenly Courts. His death as a substitution for ours is a love offering to Father God and humanity. It meets the Heavenly Realm principles of sacrifice. It aligns with the righteousness and truth thus keeping the harmony and integrity of Heaven. The sacrifice heals the breach created by Adam in his rebellion against God (1 Corinthians 15:21 – 23). Jesus gave his life.

Jesus' sacrifice was an intentional sacrifice full of love. No one took Jesus' life, he gave it. As stated in Philippians 2 5 – 8

> *5Let this mind be in you, which was also in Christ Jesus, 6who, being in the form of God, did not consider it robbery to be equal with God, 7but made Himself of no reputation, taking the form of a bondservant, and coming in the likeness of men. 8And being found in appearance as a man, He humbled Himself and became obedient to the point of death, even the death of the cross.*

Jesus Christ did not usurp the authority and majesty of God. He did not take ownership of the Glory of God, when he was in the form of humanity. This would have been the robbery. Remember, our God made humanity in his image and likeness (Genesis 1:26). Jesus Christ subjugated himself to the will of God sacrificing all he was becoming while occupying a physical body. Instead, Jesus Christ chose to be a willing servant of Father God while in his physical body. Everything Jesus was and did was placed under the dominion and authority of Father God. This is why he stated he only did and said what Father God told him to do (John 5:19 – 20). He let go of all ownership of his deeds and words. Jesus Christ sacrificed his Glory in Heavenly Realms for a spiritual living hope to be birthed in humanity. He then sacrificed everything he could be and was in the physical realm overcoming the temptation of the devil (Luke 4:1 – 13). He became the door and way for all of us to enter the Heavenly Realms while we live in a physical body. Faith, trust, obedience, surrender, and sacrifice are the truths Jesus enacted to accomplish this as the son of man. This pattern is still alive in the spiritual realm. It is still a living spiritual hope and eternal truth. The results of Jesus Christ actions are recorded in the Courts of Heaven. As in all words in heaven they are filled with spirit and truth, thus the pattern is alive for eternity. It is how we the children of God may enter into the presence of our God and commune with him while we live on this earth. Through faith we accept the gift of Jesus Christ and in love we seek Jesus Christ and the Kingdom of God.

When we seek God with all our hearts, we enter the pattern Jesus marked in the spiritual Heavenly Realms with his own blood. We are seeking God and his Kingdom. As the scripture states, we are to have the same mind of Christ and follow his spiritual footsteps into Heavenly Realms. We begin by accepting Jesus Christ as Lord as an act of faith. The act of faith is not an intellectual decision formed in the soul mind, but one of gratitude and love poured from the soul heart. It is accepting our own inability to accomplish this task by our understanding, strength and abilities.

Faith powered by love and gratitude transmutes in Heavenly Realms and becomes spiritual substance. In Heavenly Realms, this faith/surrender action leads to unity with God's righteousness. As declared in 1 Peter 2:24

who Himself bore our sins in His own body on the tree, that we,
having died to sins, might live for righteousness—by whose stripes
you were healed

The dynamics in Heavenly Realms is such that righteousness moves back and forth into living love. It transmutes into becoming and being both at the same time. This is the demonstration of the now faith, living in eternity. The offered love of the seeker becomes a recognized substance in Heavenly Realms. Faith/surrender in love becomes righteousness. This righteousness is a vehicle to enter the presence of God in a deeper, personal way. The Heavenly Realm principle of "like attracted to like" is activated. The righteousness of Jesus Christ that is birthed in the person's spiritual body is recognized in Heavenly Realms. Now a deeper communication can happen between the person seeking God and God himself. This is what Jesus meant when he said, "seek first the Kingdom of God and His Righteousness" (Matthew 6:33).

We are to return to the source of all life, the Creator of our Cosmos while in our physical forms. We are to align with the true structure or blueprint of Heavenly Realms, the basic principles underlying the Cosmos. It is in faith and love we enter this spiritual realm. We are to enter the Holy presence with a sacrifice. It is given in love and thanksgiving. Throughout the Bible God describes this pattern for those who seek God. We are not to come empty handed (Exodus 34:19 - 20). Like our God who sacrificed his best, we are taught to give our best to God. What we honor with our time, talents, and possessions demonstrates what we love.

We, the created of God, were given life. By the sacrifices of Jesus Christ we were given a new birth, an opportunity to be recreated in the likeness of Jesus Christ. Our God sacrificed their best for us to have the hope of Glory (Colossians 1:27). How do we respond to these gifts? Do we honor the giver with our best? Are we willing to sacrifice our own understanding and lives as we are known in our physical world?

When we were created God chose to give us free will. He took a great chance that we would turn to Him in thanksgiving and obedience. God allows us to come to him and seek life through him or enter into rebellion and end up in chaos and death (Deuteronomy 30:19). When all rationalizations, justifications, and arguments of the mind are stripped away this choice is what we face. We will choose:

> ➢ Enter into rebellion against the structure of the Cosmos by attempting to continue our self-focused lifestyle?
> ➢ Surrender and sacrifice self to seek God and enter Heavenly realms?

As Paul noted when he prayers for the followers of Jesus Christ in Ephesians, we are to know the greater power of the unending love of our Creator God. Ephesians 3:16 -19

> *[16]that He would grant you, according to the riches of His glory, to be strengthened with might through His Spirit in the inner man, [17]that Christ may dwell in your hearts through faith; that you, being rooted and grounded in love, [18]may be able to comprehend with all the saints what is the width and length and depth and height— [19]to know the love of Christ which passes knowledge; that you may be filled with all the fullness of God.*

This love is so precious. It is greater than any knowledge we may possess in the physical realm. When we enter the Heavenly Kingdom in faith and love we become what God intended humanity to be. The results of the process of following Jesus' spiritual pattern are to live in the fulness of God. As we walk and live in this physical world, we are filled with the fulness of God. The mandate given to us in Genesis is completed. We become fruitful and possess the Cosmos. We manifest the Kingdom of God in the Cosmos He created as it is in Heavenly Realm.

Diane M. Neumann

4

The Kingdom of God on Earth

Matthew 6:33

> *But seek first the kingdom of God and His righteousness, and all these things shall be added to you.*

Jesus is discussing with his disciples where their focus needs to be while living in this Cosmos. This discussion begins with the concept of worry and anxieties. These worries are fears based on possible futures of lack. These understandings were centered on their own opportunity and ability to provide for their own needs. Jesus is telling them do not focus on the ways and things of the world as we see them. Instead, Jesus states set your mind on the unseen Heavenly Realms knowing it is the source of all life and goodness. When we align with the original source then all that is needed or desired within the Cosmos will be provided to the seeker. Our soul minds are to seek, by faith, that which is of the Heavenly Kingdom. Jesus is describing an alternative way to live in our Cosmos. It is this original world order conceived by God that we can bring into our Cosmos and function within while living in our mortal bodies. It is found in aligning with the will of God and his authority in our lives.

The visible present world is the one we were forced into when Adam gave his authority to the devil (Genesis 3:6 – 7). It is a world defined by the Tree of Knowledge of Good and Evil. Eating of this fruit of this tree caused our connection to God through our spirit bodies to be damaged. Like Adam we were forced to rely on our physical senses and crippled soul-minds and soul-hearts to live in this alternative world. Jesus is telling his disciples to live and pray as he showed them in Matthew 6: 10

Your kingdom come. Your will be done on earth as it is in heaven.

What is being declared is the authority and power of the Heavenly Realm, (the source of all that is created within this cosmos) to overcome the world maintained through the Tree of Knowledge of Good and Evil. It is agreeing with the will of God over the will of enslaved humanity. It is a submission and obedience to the standards and practices in the Heavenly Realm over man-made standards and governance. It is choosing to align oneself to the harmony of creation.

To the Jewish listeners, the truth of the Heavenly Kingdom was real in their understanding. They were aware of two worlds and two Kingdoms. To them, the spiritual Kingdoms, or unseen world was known by signs and manifestations that were not explained by human concepts and interpretations of the natural world. Mighty works were recorded in the Bible. The covenant God made with Abraham is an eternal contract of mutual benefits between God and people. When people did their part in the covenant, God came through with his protection and provision. These were signs and miracles beyond what humanity could do on their own. When God was invited into their situations, manifestations of God's presence would change situations. Jesus was demonstrating this to them as he functioned in this Cosmos. As he stated in Luke 11:20

But if I cast out demons with the finger of God, surely the kingdom of God has come upon you.

As a Son of Man who dedicated himself to the covenant with God, Jesus was exercising his right to impose the order and truth of God over all that was functioning in disorder.

This Heavenly Realm was only unseen in a soul that had not trained to hear the voice of God. It was only unseen in the physical realm. Those who could not sense the Spiritual Heavenly Realms were still caught in the limitation of the Tree of Knowledge of Good and Evil, blinding their spiritual eyes (2 Corinthians 4:4). When a person sought God, obeyed the commandments, and surrendered their choices to God, their spirits came alive. Eyes within the spirit body and ears within the spirit body could be opened to behold this Heavenly Kingdom in visions and dreams. In this Heavenly Realm, known as an invisible world within our Cosmos, the Kingdom of God exists.

The Hebrew faith embraces the Heavenly Realms created our Cosmos (Hebrews 11:3). The greater authority was in the Spiritual Kingdom since it was the source. It had the power to overcome everything in the physical world. In other words, the original has greater authority than the copy in the Cosmos. The Bible records the word of God, documented interactions between humanity and the Kingdom of God. Prophets recorded personal interactions with the Kingdom of God and themselves. The laws governing this Heavenly Kingdom were also recorded in the writings of the prophets and priests. The historical interactions between God and his creation were also recorded. The Bible, valued by followers of Jesus Christ records many of these things. To the Israelite, this Kingdom of God is real, though not accessed with the five senses used in the physical world.

Our present Cosmos has structures of government and cultures dependent on the five senses. It is maintained by authority and power gained through the Tree of Knowledge of Good and Evil (1 John 5:19). To the Israelite, many of these other governments and their people worshipped false gods. Since they were grounded in understanding from a system Satan built, the Israelites rejected these gods. By Hebrew faith these entities being worshipped were demons. They were the spirits thrown out of Heavenly Realms with their leader Satan. These demons operated in an alternative spiritual kingdom within the unseen Heavenly Realms. They were empowered by the Kingdom of Spiritual darkness. To the believer in Jesus Christ, the Kingdom of God is a Kingdom of Light while the alternative spiritual Kingdom is a Kingdom of Darkness. Followers of Jesus Christ believe God has created a way for us to break out of the power of the Tree of Knowledge of Good and Evil and the Kingdom of Darkness. As recorded in Colossians 1:12 – 14

¹²giving thanks to the Father who has qualified us to be partakers of the inheritance of the saints in the light. ¹³He has delivered us from the power of darkness and conveyed us into the kingdom of the Son of His love, ¹⁴in whom we have redemption through His blood, the forgiveness of sins.

Bible scripture described the fall from grace of the leader of this alternative dark kingdom (Ezekiel 28:12 – 19)). As with all created beings, this leader and his followers were at one time part of the Kingdom of Light. In pride, Lucifer rebelled against the coming of humanity. He released a prophesy not in alignment with God's will. The prophecy declared that Lucifer would become the new creation to rule our Cosmos. Lucifer led the rebellion in Heavenly Light Realms. When he lost, those who followed him were also thrown out of the higher Heavenly Realms with him. As punishment, their access to higher Heavenly Realms of Light was limited. Our fourth dimension within our created Cosmos became a barrier they could not cross. It is known as time. These fallen angels are known as demons since they do not serve the will of God but the will of Lucifer. They are spiritual beings and do not have a corporate body made of earthly substances. They exist in the second heaven and in the Earthly Realm.

In rebellion to God, Lucifer (now called Satan) tempted Adam and Eve in the garden. From the beginning, Satan's purpose was to steal the power and authority given humanity and created his own kingdom on earth (Isaiah 14:12 - 20). God ruled on this rebellion by declaring a prophesy that recognized Satan in his form as the serpent. Satan had beguiled the serpent into doing his will with the promise to use the seed of the serpent to create an alternative superior being to Adam. God declared the result of the actions of Adam and Eve as recorded in Genesis 3:14 -

¹⁴So, the LORD God said to the serpent: "Because you have done this, you are cursed more than all cattle, and more than every beast of the field; On your belly you shall go, and you shall eat dust All the days of your life. ¹⁵And I will put enmity Between you and the

woman, and between your seed and her Seed; He shall bruise your
head, and you shall bruise His heel.

The product of the pact with Satan and the serpent, his seed, would be in constant battle within our Cosmos with God and his Heavenly Kingdom. Satan would work in the spiritual realm to seduce humans to work with him to create an alternative Earthly Kingdom. His goal is to bring the seed of the serpent into the cosmos as a replacement to humanity. The seed of the woman, who we know is Jesus Christ, would battle Satan in the spiritual realm and physical realm.

Fallen Lucifer was defeated by Jesus Christ during the three days beginning in the Garden of Gethsemane, through his death on the cross and his resurrection on what we call Easter (Colossians 1:13 – 22). Jesus built a church that would stand against the gates of hell to overcome the Kingdom of Satan both in the physical world and the spiritual realms (Matthew 16:18). He gave his followers the authority and power to overcome the kingdom of Satan (Matthew 16:19 & Matthew 28:18 – 20). Thus, two Spiritual Kingdoms are struggling against each other to be manifested within our Cosmos. Since Jesus Christ has reconciled everything in heaven and earth and all that is created through his actions, the results in the Spiritual Realms are already accomplished (Colossians 1:13 – 22). This current struggle is based on lies and deception since the victory is already complete. The only struggle left is for the church of Jesus Christ to occupy and enforce the victory of Jesus Christ in our Cosmos. Jesus final instructions to his disciples is recorded in Matthew 28:18 - 20

> *[18]And Jesus came and spoke to them, saying, "All authority has been given to Me in heaven and on earth. [19]Go therefore and make disciples of all the nations, baptizing them in the name of the Father and of the Son and of the Holy Spirit, [20]teaching them to observe all things that I have commanded you; and lo, I am with you always, even to the end of the age." Amen.*

Jesus empowers his followers with all his authority. In his name, the followers enforce these victories. Satan is a sore loser and refuses to accept his defeat. He knows humanity is born into the Tree of Knowledge of Good and Evil. Jesus encouraged his followers to pray for the Kingdom of God to come on earth as it is in Heavenly Realms. They are to follow the commandments of Jesus Christ and use the spiritual tools given to them to meet the original mandate of God. In Genesis God told humanity to (Gensis1:28):

> ➢ Multiply and increase in number
> ➢ Fill the entire earth and subdue it under your authority
> ➢ Rule the Cosmos as God rules in Heavenly Realms
> ➢ Seek the aid of our three-fold God and using all we are taught through them.

The followers of God are to align our Cosmos in accordance with the blueprint of its creation in Heavenly Realms. Harmony between the Heavenly Realms and our Cosmos will bring prosperity, peace and righteousness within all the Cosmos. As we choose to participate in the Covenant of Blood of Jesus Christ, God will provide protection and provision. The followers are to act. We are to battle against the creation of the alternative world Satan is trying to build.

There is a battle played out in our cosmos to create two worlds on earth. Jesus has defeated the enemy of God, Satan and his army. On one side are the demons and the followers of the occult to build the kingdom that serves and honors the spiritual dark Kingdom of Satan. Through lies, deception, and occultic activities some humans have cooperated with Satan to build an alternative world in the seen, physical world.

On the other side is the church of Jesus Christ and the authority and power of the Kingdom of God, the Creator. The church is being called to overcome the alternative world on earth through the tools and victory Jesus gave them. Thus, the prayer of Jesus declaring God's will be done and his Kingdom come on earth as it is in Heavenly Realms.

Our God is calling his followers to come forth in trust and faith. Just as he called them through John the Baptist, we are to repent of an old understanding and embrace the mindset of Jesus Christ. As stated in Romans 12:2

> *And do not be conformed to this world, but be transformed by the renewing of your mind, that you may prove what is that good and acceptable and perfect will of God.*

We are a new creation no longer under the power of the Tree of Knowledge of Good and Evil. We are free from the understanding that good and evil are equal in power and authority. Jesus Christ reconciled it all back to the original pattern. We are children of the light (1 Thessalonians 5:5). Light always overcomes darkness. We are called to live in this truth and enforce it in our regions.

When Jesus' spirit body and soul body re-entered his broken physical body, the Hoy Spirit brooded over him. The resurrection power in the physical body was activated and Jesus became a new creation. The first born of the new creation walked out of the grave. Jesus had given all his blood in sacrifice for our redemption. Now new blood, resurrection blood, is in him. We who are the followers of Jesus Christ have invited Jesus Christ into ourselves. We have surrendered our will and authority to him. Now we live in spirit in Jesus Christ, and he lives in us. As stated in Romans 8:10 -11

> *[10]And if Christ is in you, the body is dead because of sin, but the Spirit is life because of righteousness. [11]But if the Spirit of Him who raised Jesus from the dead dwells in you, He who raised Christ from the dead will also give life to your mortal bodies through His Spirit who dwells in you.*

What is true for Jesus is true for us. We are free from the power of the Tree of Knowledge of Good and evil. By the blood of Jesus we are new creations, living in Jesus and he living in us (Acts 17:28).

We enter into a process to cleanse our soul-minds of all misunderstandings born of the fruit of the Tree of Knowledge of Good and Evil. As Paul explains this understanding when he writes to the Philippians. Philippians 1:5 -6

⁵for your fellowship in the gospel from the first day until now, ⁶being confident of this very thing, that He who has begun a good work in you will complete it until the day of Jesus Christ.

As we center our wills on God's will, we align with his purposes and plans for us. As we trust God beyond that what we know in our physical world, we learn how to operate in our spiritual bodies. It is a surrender to God's will and obedience to what the Holy Spirit teaches us to do. As stated in 1 John 2: 27

But the anointing which you have received from Him abides in you, and you do not need that anyone teach you; but as the same anointing teaches you concerning all things, and is true, and is not a lie, and just as it has taught you, you will abide in Him.

Through this surrender and obedience, we find our destinies in Jesus Christ. As old patterns and understandings are broken, our spiritual bodies become alive in greater measure. When we rise in love to honor our God, we can unite with Father God through the indwelling of Jesus Christ within us. These ways of thinking and believing overcome all the attempts of the enemy of God to pull us back into the Tree of Knowledge of Good and Evil.

5

God's Plan for the

Tree of Good & Evil

It was never God's plan that humanity would be under the power of the Tree of Knowledge of Good and Evil. The Tree was placed in the Garden of Eden to serve another purpose. It was to teach obedience to God's will and Kingdom of God principles. God gave Adam and Eve every other tree. Multiple trees were given in exchange for just one given to God. God did not need this tree for his existence. Adam did not need the fruit of the Tree of Knowledge of Good and Evil for his existence. By obediently following the Kingdom of God's principles, Adam was paying homage to God. The principle is stated in Genesis 2:16

> [16]*And the LORD God commanded the man, saying, "Of every tree of the garden you may freely eat;* [17]*"but of the tree of the knowledge of good and evil you shall not eat, for in the day that you eat of it you shall surely die."*

Adam was learning to discipline his spirit under the will of God by freely surrendering to God's will. God's wisdom was greater than Adam's wisdom (Isaiah 55:8-9). When God brought life and order back into the substance of the cosmos, he separated the spiritual light from the spiritual darkness. Death, chaos and destruction were in the spiritual darkness. This tree was a balance between the two spiritual substances. God was requiring Adam to trust God's greater wisdom and depend on it rather than his own experiences. Adam's obedience was a sacrifice to demonstrate love and gratitude, like God sacrifices through love. Obedience and trust were the actions God was looking for in Adam. The tree was like the tithe (Malachi 3:10 – 12). A small percentage of what a person has is given in thanksgiving and adoration for all God gives. It is thanksgiving for life, provision, and prosperity given by God to the person. The Tree of Knowledge of Good and Evil was to be a living offering of Adam to demonstrate his love for God.

When God walked in the garden with Adam, they communicated, and God taught Adam the principles of the Kingdom of God (Genesis 2:19). God imparted higher spiritual knowledge to Adam. They communicated spirit to spirit. Being created in the image and likeness of God, Adam possessed a three-part being. The spiritual body in Adam was alive and communicated directly with God spirit to spirit. It was a sacred relationship. One would call it pure and undefiled. The relationship was God-honoring. It recognized God as creator and Adam as the created. As long as a proper honoring occurred, the balance between Heavenly Realm and the created Cosmos was maintained. Since God gave dominion of the Cosmos to Adam, it was his actions that maintained the balance (Gensis 1:28). Harmony, as shared rhythms, frequencies, and patterns between the two regions, resounded in the Cosmos.

When Adam chose to rebel against God and disobey his commandment consequences developed effecting all of humanity. The close intimate relationship with God was modified. By partaking of the Tree of Knowledge of Good and Evil the soul bodies of Adam and Eve no longer were completely holy. Both possibilities of holiness and rebellion now lived in the soul of humanity. This combination reduces the possibility of a close, intimate relationship with an absolutely good God. Knowledge of evil colors the soul with what cannot exist in Absolute Goodness. This knowledge birthed in rebellion is filled with destructive power. Instead of a pure soul with the ability to choose obedience/disobedience as an act of love, now rebellion and the means to carry it out exist in the souls of humanity. A possibility for creating an alternative world that does not honor God and serve his plans now lives in human souls. That which was separated by God when he put a barrier between the spiritual light and the spiritual darkness can now be seeded and grow within human understanding. A relationship with God where God leads through teaching self-control is replaced with a possibility of warring against God and his authority.

It was the disobedience to the laws of order and harmony that destroyed an intimate, sacred relationship. When confronted by God to admit what God already knew, Adam refused to admit his part (Genesis 3:12). He chose to blame and cunning instead. Eve chose evasion and blame rather than repentance and forgiveness offered in discussion with God (Genesis 3:13). By their own will they stood in rebellion without remorse. Guilt covered them as much as the leaves they wove for physical protection. The true fruits of the tree of Knowledge of Good and Evil had blossomed in their words and soul-hearts. Guilt, shame, regret, fear, blame, anger, and pride now lived in their soul-bodies. They turned down redemption by denying the truth. They could not come to the Absolutely Good God with denial in their souls. God was asking for truth so he could offer repentance and forgiveness. Truth underscores the foundation of all of the Cosmos. Aligning with truth allows a return to unity with God and the Heavenly Realms.

Adam admitted what now drove his thinking as stated in Genesis 3:10

> *So, he said, "I heard Your voice in the garden, and I was afraid because I was naked; and I hid myself."*

Fear developed as the result of losing the holiness that had covered Adam. This fear was a driving force in his new understanding. The holy covering, or Glory, had allowed him to live awake in his spiritual body, intimately communicating with God. The broken connection with his spiritual body bred mistrust of the Creator. Hanging onto deception rather than choosing the truth created a fear of punishment. This is another form of fear. Self-reliance is born in this fear. Pride wells up in the soul along with fear of failure. In this understanding, judgment of self and others rather than trusting God's ways and will guide personal actions. All of these attitudes and thoughts build barriers in the soul to seek God's ways and will. The spirit body no longer can influence the soul body when these attitudes and self-created barriers are supported in daily living.

From that moment on, humanity was under a different covenant with God. God sought Adam's descendants that would desire and seek a close personal relationship with God. God's goal was always to restore the intimate relationship that was destroyed in the Garden of Eden with humanity. Various agreements or covenants were struck between God and humanity to accomplish this task. Abraham lived in such a covenant as he grew in relationship with God. Moses entered a similar covenant with God seeking his direction in all God commanded him to accomplish. Moses received written decrees from the Heavenly Realm to guide human behavior. These written decrees were for building a world culture that seeks intimacy with God. They also served to protect the people from the participating in the alternative world culture outside of relationship with God. To distinguish this written covenant from the Covenant Jesus Christ created with those who make him their LORD, we call the Mosaic covenant the Covenant of the Law of Sin and Death.

Jesus Christ satisfied all the requirements from the Courts of Heaven to destroy the power of the Tree of Knowledge of Good and Evil in the human soul bodies. Humanity now has access to this freedom from the Tree of Knowledge of Good and Evil. By accepting the gift of Jesus Christ by grace and surrender to the principles of the covenant of the Blood of Jesus Christ this freedom is possible. The alternative world created through the power and submission to the Tree of Knowledge of Good and Evil is destroyed when the followers of Jesus Christ align with the Kingdom of God. As stated in John 1:17

> *For the law was given through Moses, but grace and truth came through Jesus Christ.*

Truth, the foundation of our Cosmos, written into every created entity, now can be manifested and maintained by the Sons and Daughters of God. The alignment in faith, obedience, and submission allows harmony and balance to return to earth as it is in Heavenly Realms. Unity of purpose between

Heavenly Realms and the created Cosmos is restored by Jesus Christ (Colossians 1:19 -23). It is the followers of Jesus Christ that are called to maintain and enforce this victory as stated in Matthew 16:19

> *And I will give you the keys to the kingdom of heaven, and whatever you bind on earth will be bound in heaven, and whatever you loose on earth will be loosed in heaven.*

We have legal authority through the Courts in Heavenly Realms to loose heavenly decisions, decrees, powers and authority into our Cosmos.

In every person born into this world, the soul carries the ability to know and understand both good and evil. This tree of Knowledge of Good and Evil literally lives in each person's soul body in the spiritual world. Humans can choose to seek either option. Moses records that God is telling Abraham's progeny to choose life or death by following either option (Deuteronomy 30:15- 19). Because God created human free will, this option still exists today. God is calling humanity to choose between actions that lead to death or life.

God's plan was for the soul body to be mediator between what was seen and known in the physical realm and what was seen and known through the spiritual body in the spirit realm. Adam and Eve lived in and functioned simultaneously in both realms. This ability is what was sabotaged by the enemy. When Jesus Christ satisfied the requirements of the covenant of the law of sin and death in Heavenly Realm Courts, he restored the possibility for us to become what God intended. 1 Corinthians 15: 20 - 22

> *[20] But now is Christ risen from the dead and become the first fruits of them that slept. [21] For since by man came death, by man came also the resurrection of the dead. [22] For as in Adam all die, even so in Christ shall all be made alive.*

When he walked out of the grave, resurrected Jesus Christ became the first born of the new creation. As he stated in John 11:25 - 26

²⁵Jesus said to her, "I am the resurrection and the life.
He who believes in Me, though he may die, he shall live.
²⁶"And whoever lives and believes in Me shall never die.
Do you believe this?"

By faith, Jesus Christ asks all his followers the same question. The resurrected Jesus is eternal life. The followers of Jesus Christ are invited into the process of being crucified with Christ so all we have done, thought and believed in agreement with the Tree of Knowledge of Good and Evil dies (Galatians 2:20). We seek the Kingdom of God following the patterns or footsteps of Jesus Christ in the spirit realm. We become a new creation in Christ (2 Corinthians 5:16 – 18).

Jesus Christ is living within us. As stated in Ephesians 2:

⁴But God, who is rich in mercy, because of His great love with which He loved us, ⁵even when we were dead in trespasses, made us alive together with Christ (by grace you have been saved), ⁶and raised us up together, and made us sit together in the heavenly places in Christ Jesus,

The mystery of faith is we rise into Heavenly Realms through the door or way that is the resurrected Jesus Christ (John 14:6). We do this while living in our earthly bodies. His presence lives within our soul bodies as it states we are together with Jesus Christ. As noted, the spirits of fear live in the souls, so may the spirit of truth live in our souls. Paul is also showing the other side. We actually gave our lives to Jesus to rise in his resurrection. Just as we bond through our souls with others, so now part of our soul lives in Jesus Christ in Heavenly Realms. We were raised up together to sit in Christ Jesus.

As new creations we are living in this Cosmos in our physical bodies and our spiritual bodies. We are alive in the spirit realm and fully functioning in both the physical realm and spiritual realm. A pact or covenant is offered. Die to self and accept me as Lord and I will give you eternal life as you follow and obey me. The self that is to die is the one that was created through the Knowledge of the Tree of Good and Evil. It is cleansing all the attitudes, behaviors, thoughts, emotions, and habits created as barriers to God within the soul body. As stated in Hebrews 8:10

> *[10] "For this is the covenant that I will make with the house of Israel after those days, says the LORD: I will put my laws in their mind and write them on their hearts; and I will be their God, and they shall be My people. [11] "None of them shall teach his neighbor, and none his brother, saying, 'Know the LORD,' for all shall know Me, from the least of them to the greatest of them. [12] "For I will be merciful to their unrighteousness, and their sins and their lawless deeds I will remember no more." [13] In that He says, "A new covenant," He has made the first obsolete. Now what is becoming obsolete and growing old is ready to vanish away.'*

Those who accept Jesus Christ as Lord and savior willingly subjugate their choices to God. They accept all that Jesus Christ has done as a gift, not earned, but given to them by God. It is God's part of covenant, a return to righteous status with God. Their part of covenant is to surrender their lives, their choices, and futures to God in love and obedience. It is a total commitment to the authority and will of God. Simply stated it is obediently following the written word of God, trusting God's will and ways above what is seen and known in human understanding. As stated in Romans 5:19

> *For as by one man's disobedience many were made sinners, so also by one Man's obedience many will be made righteous.*

As a gift, Jesus Christ completed and ended the separation from God. In essence, accepting the gift, by embracing Covenant of the Blood of Jesus is choosing to return to the Garden of Eden relationship with God.

The believers may now enter the process of becoming the sons and daughters of God fully awake in the spirit realm and the physical realm as they live on earth (John 1:12). In the mature follower of Jesus Christ, the Tree of Knowledge of Good and Evil is destroyed. It is what is meant when the believer declares in faith the verses in Galatians 2:20

"I have been crucified with Christ; it is no longer I who live, but Christ lives in me; and the life which I now live in the flesh I live by faith in the Son of God, who loved me and gave Himself for me."

The power and authority of the Tree of Knowledge of Good and Evil is annihilated. The debt has been paid. Under the covenant of the blood of Jesus Christ the believer has agreed to become the living temple of God. This surrender of self and uniting in greater measure with the truth of Jesus Christ allows resurrected life to pervade the spirit and soul bodies of a believer. It is a daily process. Submitting and following the patterns and will of God over self-centered lifestyles tears apart the roots and branches of the Tree of Knowledge of Good and Evil that grew in the soul body. Resurrection power and authority in Jesus Christ trumps all power in the Tree of Knowledge of Good and Evil. Spiritual wisdom can overtake soul wisdom created in the Tree of Knowledge of Good and Evil. Now the believer can break the power of the enemy of God that was ruling in rebellion in the soul body when operating only in human wisdom.

6

Sacrifice of Self: An Action of Love

Mathew 16: 24 - 26

> *24Then Jesus said to His disciples, "If anyone desires to come after Me, let him deny himself, and take up his cross, and follow Me. 25For whoever desires to save his life will lose it, but whoever loses his life for my sake will find it. 26For what profit is it to a man if he gains the whole world, and loses his own soul? Or what will a man give in exchange for his soul?"*

In two other Gospels, the same words are written. (Mark 8:24 & Luke 9:23). This witness of three emphasizes the spiritual law in these statements. These directions are important for understanding a principle within Heavenly Kingdom Realms.

The Jewish people who followed Jesus, understood Jesus spoke of a Spiritual Kingdom. As previously mentioned, the reality of two spiritual Kingdoms competing for control of the Jewish nation was evident to them. The listener understood the life being lost or saved was the temporal life, within the physical body. The reference to gain the whole world was a key to them. It signaled that Jesus is talking about working to maintain the physical temporal body and its comfort. They believed the essence of a person who lived beyond death was held in the soul. The ways of the world were known. The covenant with Moses and God was the Jewish understanding on how to seek an alternative world standard while living in the physical world. This covenant relationship was a method of aligning with the original authority in the Heavenly Kingdom Realm. Yet, many knew they failed at maintaining the covenant. Some Jewish people also saw those in leadership whose words and actions did not match the requirements of covenant. These two groups were the targeted audience of Jesus. The observers were looking for another way to align with Heavenly Kingdom Realm authority and power while living in this Cosmos.

God's plans are to overcome the wisdom of the world fostered in the Tree of Knowledge of Good and Evil and its temptation. God is seeking those who are willing to turn their backs and efforts from human wisdom to build prosperity within the structures of the temporal world. As it is recorded in 1 Corinthians 2:1:21

> *For since, in the wisdom of God, the world through wisdom did not know God, it pleased God through the foolishness of the message preached to save those who believe.*

As mentioned earlier, the pathway into this greater wisdom of God was through faith and not our own abilities. Those whose focus is on the temporal world do not operate in the spirit (1 Corinthians 2:14). Only in faith is the doorway to the spiritual realm open (Romans 1:17). Denying self-independency and human wisdom is the first sacrifice of each person to enter into the greater Heavenly Realms. As Jesus stated it is a willingness to be crucified (Galatians 2:20). All that we have known, depended on, used to evaluate choices, and actions are to be placed on the cross of Jesus.

Jesus is the lamb that was slain for the propitiation of our sins (1 John 2:2). It satisfied the Court of Heaven's requirement to break humanity out of the power of the Tree of Knowledge of Good and Evil and return us to our original relationship with God. As Jesus stood in the gap paying the price through sacrifice, we are asked to also sacrifice to accept the gift. It is a surrender, and a self-sacrifice as noted in Ephesians 2:8 – 9

⁸For by grace you have been saved through faith, and that not of yourselves; it is the gift of God, ⁹not of works, lest anyone should boast.

This is the total surrender and willingness to grant to Jesus Christ the lordship of one's life. As Jesus stated, our actions are gifts we initiate to honor Jesus Christ. We choose to die to self.

This is the first sacrifice of the followers of Jesus Christ. Like our God it is an act of love. Only in gratitude and love will this choice stand against the attacks of the enemy to strip a person of this new commitment. As noted in 1 Corinthians 13:5 -6: Love is not self-seeking nor is it proud. Love does not delight in doing wrong. This acceptance of freedom from the power and authority of the Tree of Good and Evil is through a surrender of self-focus. It is raising up Jesus Christ to be first love in one's life. Only actively participating in this living spiritual love can one conquer the temptation of pride. There is no way fear can overtake a person who abides in the love for God (1 John 4:18). This love shatters all mind accepted loyalty to God for what Jesus Christ accomplished. A soul heart that now views all through the acts of Jesus can overcome the temptations of the world. As stated in 1 John 4:16 (NIV)

And so, we know and rely on the love God has for us. God is love. Whoever lives in love lives in God, and God in them.

As we remain in our love for God, the presence of Jesus Christ overtakes our soul hearts. This is why John states in 1 John 3:9

Whoever has been born of God does not sin, for His seed remains in him; and he cannot sin, because he has been born of God.

It is the presence of Jesus in our souls, which is nurtured in worship and mutual love that grows this seed. By allowing the lordship of God to overtake and guide this process, we continually sacrifice ourselves to God in this act of love. Our desire is to present a holy and pure love to the one who is love.

How we achieve this growing of the seed is the meaning of Pauls' prayer for the believer as recorded in Ephesians 1: 17-18 (NIV)

> [17]*I keep asking that the God of our Lord Jesus Christ, the glorious Father, may give you the Spirit of wisdom and revelation, so that you may know him better.* [18]*I pray that the eyes of your heart may be enlightened in order that you may know the hope to which he has called you, the riches of his glorious inheritance in his holy people,*

As noted in an earlier chapter the condition of the heart is measured by our God and has consequences in our relationship with our God. As we worship and surrender ourselves to God, he shows us what still remains in our soul of the Tree of Knowledge of Good and Evil. The Holy Spirit then convicts us of how to remove it (1 John 3:19 – 22).

In true spiritual love, the giver of love believes the object of love has greater worth than the one who loves. Love is the gift and the sacrifice. Living spiritual love is an action and a substance. It is alive and blended together. This living spiritual love is just like it is in Heavenly Realms, as explained in quantum understanding. Loving, giving, and sacrifice move together and yet have substance/form. What is created in the act of loving is greater than the individuals who are participating in the loving. In worship, gratitude is given to God. These are the seeds of love planted in faith in the heart of the worshipper. Spiritual living love blooms in this unity.

Those who understand the price Jesus paid, and what is required by the receiver are overwhelmed with the love of God. Only in choosing the death of self can this love from God and for God be embraced. These actions occur in the soul hearts of the followers of Jesus Christ. The action releases a unity of a human spirit speaking and uniting with spirit of God in Heavenly Realms.

For this to happen the spiritual eyes of the followers of Jesus Christ stay focused on King Jesus. The desires of the world are to be subjugated to this living spiritual love. All temptations of the physical world are born of desires. John explains this in 1 John 2:15 – 17

> *[15]Do not love the world or the things in the world. If anyone loves the world, the love of the Father is not in him. [16]For all that is in the world— the lust of the flesh, the lust of the eyes, and the pride of life— is not of the Father but is of the world. [17]And the world is passing away, and the lust of it; but he who does the will of God abides forever.*

The two competing world views are expressed by John. If we place our first love in Father God, then through the Blood Covenant of Jesus Christ, God will provide and meet our desires. If we choose to seek the world view and choose to meet our own desires within this understanding, then we will not hold onto the love for Father God.

The third view is to believe in Jesus Christ as the son of God and give him loyalty, but not to trust him to satisfy all of our desires. This is based on a mindset that agrees with the principles of Jesus Christ as the son of God but lacks the love commitment to God. In this mindset there is always a trust issue waiting to see if God will do what he says. It is not a complete trust that God is and will always complete what he has said (Isaiah 55:11). Only in a living spiritual love is it possible to embrace this type of trust. This distrust breeds doubt and a double-minded relationship with God. James describes this double-minded condition (James 1:7). Such a person becomes plagued with desires and confused on how to achieve peace with God. Loyalty cannot stand up to the wiles of the enemy. Surrender to God is not complete when one is only loyal. Again, as stated in the definition of love, delighting in satisfying pleasures outside of covenant with God is betrayal of God. Enjoyment is found in the wrongdoing. It opens doors in one's soul for lust to overpower the soul. This can lead to bringing back the power of the Tree of Knowledge of Good and Evil in a person's life.

Jesus, as the Son of Man, was well aware of the draw of desires within the soul. He sought Father God and his love to conquer these desires. Jesus applied all the teaching of the Prophets and the Covenant of the Law given by Moses to his life. He sought the Kingdom of God with these tools. Jesus entered deeply into loving God above all else. When he faced his forty days in the desert, he was tempted in his soul to turn away from this covenant. The Bible records three of these temptations. In each encounter, Jesus answers with the Word of God. This is the living, spiritual truth that overcomes all darkness. He had it embedded into his soul, heart, mind, and will. Later, he tells his disciples the key to overcoming these desires in the soul. It is recorded in Luke 12:29 -32

> *[29]And do not seek what you should eat or what you should drink, nor have an anxious mind. [30]For all these things the nations of the world seek after, and your Father knows that you need these things. [31]But seek the kingdom of God, and all these things shall be added to you. [32]Do not fear, little flock, for it is your Father's good pleasure to give you the kingdom.*

Jesus clearly states to trust God above what is seen in the visible world. We are to change our mind's focus that centers on lack. Anxious thoughts are governed by the mind of someone who depends on self to solve most situations. Notice he is highlighting again humanity's systems, nations, versus the Kingdom of God. Trust and know God first and seek him. Then the creator of all and the sustainer of all life in our Cosmos will provide. The provisions come from the original source of all life.

When we live in the Tree of Knowledge of Good and Evil, we become the captain of our own souls. We judge and evaluate what is good and true based on our own experiences and human wisdom. In this condition, the spirit body is not fully functional. Through Moses, God gave the Israelites the Law and Commandments to mediate human wisdom. This was not the final solution, but a step to breaking free of the power of the Tree of Knowledge of Good an Evil. As recorded in Romans 3:20

> *Therefore, by the deeds of the law no flesh will be justified in His sight, for by the law is the knowledge of sin.*

The law was a tool to teach humanity in their own efforts, they could not achieve righteousness. It was to define sin and identify the process of building sin in one's soul. Rightoeusness is necessary to align with the Heavenly Kingdom Realm and maintain optimum life while living in this Cosmos. Sin within the soul separates humanity from God. When we choose Jesus Christ as our Lord, we are ceding our dead self to him to resurrect in his righteousness. By grace we are no longer caught in the power of the Tree of Knowledge of Good and Evil.

The covenantal exchange of sacrificing self for the righteousness of Jesus Christ permits the record in the Courts of Heaven of Jesus Christ to legally satisfying the breaking of the power of the Tree of Knowledge of Good and Evil to become our own. When we follow the pathway Jesus Christ created in our Cosmos and is recorded in Heavenly Realms, we are no longer fighting our desires in our soul bodies. Desires will always tantalize the soul of humanity. Under covenantal agreement, we are applying the mind and heart of Jesus Christ to our desires. We are capturing every thought and putting it under the blood of Jesus (2 Corinthians 10:5). When we love God, with our whole hearts, minds, and wills, we are activating the authority and power of the resurrection blood of Jesus to align those desires with the perfect will of God. Since Jesus Christ has won all the battles to destroy the power of the Tree of Knowledge of Good and Evil, we are applying those victories to our own lives. As John states, the act of love drives us to purify ourselves. 1 John 3:3

> *And everyone who has this hope in Him purifies himself, just as He is pure.*

Capturing and subjugating these desires to this covenant of the Blood of Jesus is a process of sacrifice. We continually surrender the desires to God so He may meet our needs. We are breaking agreement with every past way these desires were satisfied if they were met outside of the principles of the Heavenly Realms. These further sacrifices become love offerings to God.

As we grow in our daily relationship with God, we seek him and his Kingdom through Jesus Christ. Following the example of Jesus Christ, we give honor and praise to our God for who he is. We seek his Heavenly Kingdom and his righteousness. In faith and love for God, we surrender our day and lives to be a living sacrifice to our God. This is our part of the covenant.

7

Altars For God

God is seeking an intimate relationship with followers of his son, Jesus Christ. We enter into a covenant relationship with God when we surrender our lives to God through the grace offered by Jesus Christ. When a person makes this commitment, the covenant is recorded in the Heavenly Courts for eternity. Jesus Christ becomes our king and receives our allegiance. Jesus Christ becomes our Lord over all our actions and thoughts. We are required to account for these actions to our King. Covenant is a legal agreement. Jesus Christ paid the court costs with his life. We receive the benefits of the court action by our word of agreement. It is awarded by the grace of God, not earned through our actions. We, the followers, promise our lives to serve and honor God above all else. Our God pledges protection and provision as his part of the covenant. God is a jealous God who guards this commitment for our own protection (Deuteronomy 4:23 - 24). When God gives us directions, and commandments he is acting within this covenant agreement. Through his written word, the Bible, God also gives us patterns, tools, and methods to live the abundant life Jesus promises (John 10:10). The nature of our God is revealed in his written word, the Bible. As we operate in this covenant relationship, we seek to know who God is. There are many aspects to God.

One of the attributes of our God is He is love (1 John 4:8). As noted earlier, this love is the energy that forms the foundation of our Cosmos. God has created a pathway for his people to enter his presence to celebrate and rejoice in their freedom from the Tree of Knowledge Good and Evil. The place God anointed for these celebrations are altars. He taught those who seek him with all their hearts to build altars. One of the builders of altars was Abraham. These altars were for worship and communication with God.

Abraham built his first altar when God gave land to him and his descendants (Genesis 12:7). Abram built an additional altar in Bethal when Abram desired to communicate with God (Gensis 12:8). After traveling to Egypt and returning, Abram again sought God by building a third altar in Hebron (Genesis 13:18). His final altar was for the sacrifice of his son, as God commanded at Mount Horeb (Genesis 22:9). Each of the four altars represent stages in building an intimate relationship with God. At each altar an exchange happens. Abraham is sacrificing something different at each one.

There is a mutual giving and receiving at the altars to God. Beginning with the gift of land and a thanksgiving offering, Abram sought God at his altar. God provided and Abram acknowledged receiving the gift. As Moses later admonished his people, if we seek God with our whole heart, he will be found (Deuteronomy 4:29). The beginning relationship honored at the first altar is seeking in love and thanksgiving the presence of God. God gave a gift of provision and Abraham gave thanksgiving. He surrendered his ownership of his actions by recognizing God led him to the land. Abraham blessed God by honoring the giver. The second altar was a marker as Abram progressed in the land, he still sought the presence and wisdom of God. In the physical journey and daily living actions, Abraham again is recognizing the hand of God in guiding, providing, and protecting him. In a covenantal act, Abraham is noticing the provision of God in his own daily work. This is a surrender to the Lordship of God over his daily life. It is honoring God for being present with Abraham in the life journey. The third altar was built at Hebron after separating himself from Lot. After giving up land to Lot, God blessed the land Abram chose and promised him this land and many offsprings. Abram's faithfulness is demonstrated in him always building an altar to communicate with God. God recognized Abraham's commitment and trust in God when he separated himself from Lot. Greater dependency on God was marked at the altar. The worship at the third altar is deeper than the previous ones. Here Abram is placing his will and trust in God above not only a person's work, but also his family. Strife was occurring between Lot's people and Abraham's people. To bring peace, Abraham cut ties with his last close family member. God knew then Abraham's priorities were trusting God above himself and family opinions. As Abraham's physical journey covers the lands, his spiritual journey is marked by these different altars.

The final altar is an act of complete trust and obedience with God. Abraham had bonded in faith with God through this land/spiritual journey. Abraham has spiritually separated himself unto God. At the final altar, Abraham walks in greater faith trusting God has a solution to what he is being required to sacrifice. His only son, Isaac, is the promised child to build the nation God has declared is Abraham's inheritance. Abraham trusts God's words above the evidence he is seeing of the possible death of his son. As noted in Romans 5:17b

> *(as it is written, "I have made you a father of many nations") in the presence of Him whom he believed— God, who gives life to the dead and calls those things which do not exist as though they did.*

Abraham trusted God could bring life back to that which died. Abraham's history with God has developed a complete trust that God will uphold his covenant. He is trusting the word of God over the temptation of fear. He told the two men he left on the plains that he and his son would return after they worshipped (Gensis 22:6). Our loving God stays Abraham's hand and spares his son Isaac. God provides the lamb for sacrifice. God upholds his covenant of provision and protection. Now together God, Abraham, and Isaac may celebrate the demonstration of obedience and faith between them at this altar. Furthermore, God declared Abraham righteous. This is an eternal reward for his service to God. As later declared in Romans 8:28

> *And we know that all things work together for good to those who love God, to those who are the called according to His purpose.*

In covenant God is the provider and protector. This pattern of seeking God, honoring him through worship and altars of thanksgiving, faith, trust, and obedience are written in the eternal truths held in Heavenly Realms. This pattern is spiritually alive. It is recorded in Heavenly Courts as a living truth. As it is in Heavenly Realms is now recorded in the earthly realm. Those who follow the pattern while alive in the Cosmos have access to the blessings of this spiritual truth.

God reminded his people through his leader Joshua for another purpose of altars. They are to be memorials to events honoring God's actions as God completes his part of the covenant. When God parted the Jordan River so the Israelites could enter the promise land, he told Joshua to build an altar (Joshua 4:1 – 2). Each tribe chose a stone from the middle of the Jordan River to build this altar. The corporate unity of the tribes as God's people is expressed in this altar. They took the stones from the middle of the river. The stones become spiritually an emblem of the commitment of the people to their part of the covenant. Spiritually speaking, in the middle of our need, God acts his part of our covenant with him. We activate this by seeking God in our seasons of need at his altar. Just as stones were sought then placed as a memorial, in our times of need we are to place our weighty situations in God's hands. The people were to teach their children this story of the demonstration of God's provision and protection (Joshua 4:6 – 7). Thus, the altars now are more than a personal meeting place for a follower of God. It is a corporate gathering to remember and honor God. In seasons of need, God's people are to remember, in the middle of their situations, he provides and protects. In worship at the altars, we give honor as we remember how God has previously provided for us. We sacrifice our own ways and answers to situations and ask God to once again intercede in our lives. We let go of anxiety as well as our own solutions as an offering to God. Like Abraham, we trust God's words and promises in greater faith than what we are seeing in the physical world and personal situations. It is a trust in the spiritual covenant with God.

On this side of the cross of Jesus, his followers speak of testimonies of what God has accomplished in their lives. These are our memorials we bring to build the altars of thanksgiving and honor for our God. These testimonies are our stones we use to build a living altar for our God. Corporately these testimonies are shared to build other believers trust in God's covenant. This altar is a place where God resides when we seek him in praise and worship (Psalm 148). We connect through our relationship with Jesus Christ, spirit to spirit. It is a spiritually alive place where covenant promises are enacted by us and our God. This living altar of faith is a communication center in spiritual realms. We interact with God spirit to spirit and faith to faith. As stated in Revelation 12:10 -11:

> *¹⁰Then I heard a loud voice saying in heaven, "Now salvation, and strength, and the kingdom of our God, and the power of His Christ have come, for the accuser of our brethren, who accused them before our God day and night, has been cast down." ¹¹And they overcame him by the blood of the Lamb and by the word of their testimony, and they did not love their lives to the death.*

We the followers of Jesus Christ overcome the alternative world the enemy wants to impose through the Tree of Good and Evil by going to these altars of God. We seek his face in love and gratitude for all Jesus Christ has accomplished and given to us. At the altars, like those before us, we come to celebrate our God. We seek both individually and corporately time to honor and praise him. We seek his wisdom at his altars. We surrender our concerns and issues to God trusting in his covenant promises of protection and provision. We seek God's presence to unite with the one who is love. We give our love to our God for all He is. We celebrate the freedom we have from the Tree of Knowledge of Good and Evil. We give thanks to Jesus Christ. We honor Jesus Christ for his blood. The pattern of truth written through Abraham in Heavenly Realms is activated. This is why the Bible says in faith, we are the children of Abraham. We now can declare the Kingdom of God in our Cosmos and enforce the Heavenly Realms plans and purposes in our Cosmos.

As overcomers of this alternative world Satan is trying to create in our Cosmos we share in the righteousness of Jesus Christ (Galatians 2:20). As we rise in spiritual Heavenly Realms, we may enter the throne room of God. As stated in Hebrews 4:16

Let us therefore come boldly to the throne of grace, that we may obtain mercy and find grace to help in time of need.

We may now participate in the exchange with our God through his covenant. We offer our own understanding, our emotional baggage, and our limited solutions to our God. As stated in Proverbs 3:5 – 7

⁵Trust in the LORD with all your heart and lean not on your own understanding; ⁶In all your ways acknowledge Him, And He shall direct your paths. ⁷Do not be wise in your own eyes; Fear the LORD and depart from evil.

We surrender all to God asking for his Grace of protection and provision to supply our needs. Like Abraham, we believe God will provide. God's grace and mercy is poured into us.

8

Completing Our Mission

Using Kingdom Authority in Our Cosmos

Our love for God, as Jesus Christ loved God, sustains us. Jesus prayed we, his followers would be one just as Father God and Jesus are one (John 17:23). The unity we enjoy with God through the Blood Covenant with Jesus is to be a corporate unity. He further prayed in John 17:23

> *I in them, and You in Me; that they may be made perfect in one, and that the world may know that You have sent Me, and have loved them as You have loved Me.*

The living spiritual love of God is to consume his followers to the point the life we live will be noted as different from what the alternative life Satan is attempting to develop in our Cosmos. The followers are to function as one body. Jesus Christ is the head and of this body (Colossians 1:18). We operate under his authority in all we do.

We remain in Jesus Christ active in our part of the covenant. As stated in the previous chapters, spiritual tools of trust, faith, obedience, and surrender align us with the will of God. Jesus Christ becomes the way, the truth, and the light of God living in us. He gives us access to enter Heavenly Realms. As John states in 1 John 5:14 - 15

[14]Now this is the confidence that we have in Him, that if we ask anything according to His will, He hears us. [15]And if we know that He hears us, whatever we ask, we know that we have the petitions that we have asked of Him.

The process of entering into God's will and staying in his will has been explained in earlier chapters. Accomplishing this a precursor to operating in our Cosmos under the divine authority of King Jesus, our Lord.

Mature followers of King Jesus are now able to complete the original purpose of humanity in this Cosmos. As God stated in Genesis 1:28

Then God blessed them, and God said to them, "Be fruitful and multiply; fill the earth and subdue it; have dominion over the fish of the sea, over the birds of the air, and over every living thing that moves on the earth."

Under the authority and power of our God we can now declare the will of God to subdue our Cosmos. Under the authority of King Jesus, we can align our Cosmos with the Heavenly Realms. The key is to apply the prayer of Jesus Christ as recorded in John 17. We are to move in unity, fulfilling the multiplying requirement under the head of King Jesus. In our own strength and wisdom, the Church has not been united in love. Doctrinal differences bred in soul mind understanding have created these divisions. These are products of the Tree of Knowledge of Good and Evil for they are founded in judgment. We fall victim to what is recorded in 1 John 2:9 – 10

[9]He who says he is in the light, and hates his brother, is in darkness until now. [10]He who loves his brother abides in the light, and there is no cause for stumbling in him.

Only in submitting to King Jesus in love can we destroy all the fruit of the Tree of Knowledge of Good and Evil attempting to corrupt the Church. Maintaining our first love in Jesus Christ keeps our spiritual eyes on King Jesus. Seeking his heart to consume our soul heart stabilizes us as we relate to fellow believers. Thank God Jesus demonstrated through his teaching with his disciples how to accomplish this task!

The Pattern

As recorded in Matthew 10:1(NIV)

> *Jesus called his twelve disciples to him and gave them **authority** to drive out impure spirits and to heal every disease and sickness.*

The word "authority" in this passage is the Greek word "exousia". It is described in Strong's number G1849. Generally, it is translated as power, yet it has a broader meaning. Strong also uses it to be inclusive of the power of authority (influence) and of right (privilege). When studied from the old-world understanding, a disciple had authority under the teacher (master) to complete all designated tasks in the name of the teacher. The ones representing their master teacher had the privilege to act as the master. In spiritual terms this means to call forth actions from Heavenly Realms with the same power and authority of the master, Jesus Christ. Jesus Christ is the Lord of those who have surrendered their will and life to him. When we, his people, align with the will of God, we have the authority and power to complete the same tasks Jesus delegated to his original disciples. We have been given authority under the Blood Covenant with Jesus Christ to act in his name.

In Matthew 28:18 – 20, the risen Jesus Christ gave authority and assignments to be completed by those who chose to make Jesus Lord of their lives. As it is recorded in the NIV translation:

> *[18]Then Jesus came to them and said, "All authority in heaven and on earth has been given to me. [19]Therefore, go and make disciples of all nations, baptizing them in the name of the Father and of the Son and of the Holy Spirit, [20]and teaching them to obey everything I have commanded you. And surely, I am with you always, to the very end of the age."*

Jesus was sending his people into the world with his mission under his power and authority. As their Lord, those who aligned with Jesus and submitted to the will of God could go and complete the assignment of their Lord. Jesus was stating, nothing was strong enough, nor had the authority to overrule

Lord Jesus. Everything in our Cosmos was under the power and authority of Lord Jesus (Colossians 1:15 -20). Despite what those in rebellion to God want to believe, Jesus defeated their source of strength, the devil. The living eternal King Jesus Christ still has all authority and power. As a result of his death and resurrection Jesus' authority is recorded in Heavenly Courts (Hebrews 1:3). His victory is passed to his believers who walk in faith and surrender to his Lordship through the Covenant of the Blood of Jesus.

Lord Jesus' disciples were now to go to all nations and enforce the authority and place these nations under the authority of Lord Jesus. The critical assignment was to teach all who surrender to Lord Jesus to obey all Jesus Christ had demonstrated and taught his disciples to do. One of those activities was teaching. Before his crucifixion, disciples were sent in pairs to act in Jesus' authority demonstrating the presence of the Kingdom of God in our Cosmos (Luke 9:1 – 6). Assignments were given when Jesus sent his people out to act in his place and to drive out impure spirits and healing the sick of all diseases. In other words, they were sent to release complete deliverance, and total healing, just as Jesus himself accomplished. Matthew records the pattern to accomplish this under the will of Lord Jesus.

The first step is an admonition. Matthew 10:6 states

> *Go rather to the lost sheep of Israel.*

The disciples were to seek those lost. In Matthew 18:12 – 14, Jesus describes these lost sheep in a parable. He claims that Father God desires to leave those which are safe and seek the one that is missing. The disciples are being sent to those who have wandered off into the alternative worldview fostered by Satan. They have walked outside of the care and support of the Shepherd and his covenant. In terms of the Jewish nation, those being sought had placed themselves outside of covenant with God.

The second step was how to approach the lost. As stated in Matthew 10:7

> *As you go, proclaim this message: 'The kingdom of heaven has come near.'*

We his modern disciples are called to speak to those who lack hope and are separated from God. Our message is the Gospel declaring the Kingdom of God is near and seeking them. Since the disciples are speaking to those who were raised under the law of Covenant, they know about the Kingdom of God. The idea of God seeking them out was foreign to those who saw themselves as lost. Their religious mindset only understood punishment for sins committed. Many today have been taught similar understandings as they live in the world Satan has patterned. This seeking of God for them and then providing healing, which was forgiveness of sins in their understanding, is beyond their hope and belief. The original disciples were preaching before the resurrection of Lord Jesus. Today, for the people of God who honor Lord Jesus as King, we have a greater promise to give the lost. By preaching the Kingdom of God we bring salvation and the opportunity to enter the Kingdom of God by the blood of Jesus. This salvation is given by grace. God intended this message of the Kingdom of Heaven coming near, to be a beginning of a renewed relationship with His Kingdom and the personhood of God.

When the people of God move to the next step described in this section of Matthew, the manifestation of God's kingdom is seen. Matthew 10:8(NIV) states

> *Heal the sick, raise the dead, cleanse those who have leprosy, and drive out demons. Freely you have received; freely give.*

The great commission listed in Matthew 28:18 – 20, includes teaching and doing all Jesus did. Jesus stated to his disciples in John 14:12(NIV) his disciples would do greater works than himself because he goes to Father God.

> *Very truly, I tell you, whoever believes in Me will do the works I have been doing, and they will do even greater things than these, because I am going to the Father.*

The key is to function in faith, trust, surrender and obedience to Jesus as Lord and Master. We rise up into the Heavenly Realms and declare alignment with the blueprint in Heavenly Realms. We declare the living truth in the words of God. Under the authority of our King, we call alignment in our Cosmos as it is in Heavenly Realms. It is operating in a faith beyond what is seen in the natural world or understood at the soul-mind level. The disciples understood it was not in their own strength they were going out to the people. They trusted Jesus Christ and rested in his love. Their faith was in the authority of their master, Jesus Christ. The signs and miracles accomplished in obedience are verification that the disciple is speaking truth about God. These manifestations demonstrate that the Kingdom of God has arrived (Matthew 12:28). It is through the faith, obedience, and trust of the believer in Jesus Christ that allows the healing power of God to flow into situations. The faith and trust of the believer is in Jesus Christ who enforces his victory over all the demonic world. Authority and power are manifested through faith, obedience, and submission to the authority of Jesus Christ.

God's plan of redemption begins at salvation, yet it is complete as his children become mature in Jesus Christ. 1Peter 2:9 (NIV) states it this way:

> *But you are a chosen people, a royal priesthood, a holy nation, God's special possession, that you may declare the praises of him who called you out of darkness into his wonderful light.*

God is calling his people to be holy as God is holy. Salvation is the beginning of the process. Sanctification is the next step. Deliverance is this process of sanctification described in Matthew 10:8. As Jesus states in the Lord's prayer, "deliverance from evil". Coming out of the darkness of the world, is leaving evil behind and entering the light of truth, which is the presence of God. The followers of Jesus Christ who seek him above all are resting in the love of God and sharing in it in communion with God.

The next key in verse eight is given when it states, we have freely received, so we are to freely give. It is not by our work, or our own understanding, we have been set free. It is by God's grace, that no one can take ownership in their salvation. Just as the apostles knew their authority came from resting under Jesus' authority and not their own effort, we the people of God are required to have the same attitude. Owning the results of the cleansing of other people from demon oppression is a trap the enemy of God has set for the believers. It can feed pride, which is a tool of demons. This can open doors into the souls of the followers of Jesus Christ. Just as Jesus took private time away from his work to spend intimate time with God, it is essential the people of God frequently spend time alone with God. We are to nurture the living spiritual love with our God. Only in an intimate relationship filled with thanksgiving and praise does the person stay in right relationship with God. As noted in earlier chapters, the sharing of love during times of intimacy with God shores up the soul of the person. It is a time of surrendering to God and seeking his will. These actions aid in freely giving to others what we ourselves have received.

When walking in faith, believing God will provide, Jesus told his disciples to not take provisions with them. This is the next step in the process of operating under Kingdom Authority. As stated in Matthew 10:9 – 10

> [9]*"Provide neither gold nor silver nor copper in your money belts,*
> [10]*nor bag for your journey, nor two tunics, nor sandals, nor staffs;*
> *for a worker is worthy of his food."*

When operating under the authority of Jesus Christ, our faith leads us, not our planning. It is a slippery slope the enemy builds trying to lead God's people back into dependency on the world rather than God. It opens doors to the Tree of Knowledge of Good and Evil. We can become double-minded relying on our own strength and judgment rather than trusting God's will. When mature believers trust in the authority of Jesus Christ over all of their lives, then they possess a different mindset than those who rely on their own abilities and strengths. As mentioned earlier in the text of Matthew, these disciples were sent in pairs. Their support in each other was to help uphold their faith. Their reliance was on their master Jesus Christ. They were trusting what they had seen under Jesus Christ's authority. If Jesus stated something would happen a certain way, it did. Jesus told them their needs would be covered by God. Walking in faith requires a trusting in God so one does not regress into leaning into their own understanding (Proverbs 3:4 – 5).

Today, the mature believer requires the same kind of faith and trust. We are to seek God for direction in prayer and God's word. This word is found in the Bible, given through prophets, or revealed by Holy Spirit in visions and dreams. Seeking God's will is basic to staying under the Covenant of the Blood of Jesus. Just as Jesus continued to seek time alone with God, so the mature believers need a daily re-fill of the intimate presence of God in their daily lives. Surrendering to what God directs in this time of prayer and intimacy leads to spiritual wisdom. Choosing obedience as a response to this spiritual wisdom develops spiritual organs in the spiritual body. As stated in earlier chapters, all of this is to be wrapped in living spiritual love.

Jesus states to his disciples in John 14:21

> *21 "He who has My commandments and keeps them, it is he who loves Me. And he who loves Me will be loved by My Father, and I will love him and manifest Myself to him."*

Again, Jesus repeats the statement in John 15:10

> *"If you keep My commandments, you will abide in My love, just as I have kept My Father's commandments and abide in His love."*

Jesus abided in his Father God when he walked this earth. The fulfillment of the promise of the presence of Jesus Christ's fullness in us as his people is the result of our complete obedience and surrender to God. Just as Jesus was with Father God, we may be with him. These verses, Matthew chapter ten, verse five through ten provide the first five steps in the process of functioning within Kingdom Authority.

The next section of instructions given by Jesus to his disciples about operating under the authority of Jesus Christ relates to living within the peace that passes understanding. Jesus promised his disciples he would give them peace. As stated in John 14:27

"Peace, I leave with you, my peace I give to you; not as the world gives do I give to you. Let not your heart be troubled, neither let it be afraid."

When the resurrected Jesus Christ appeared to his disciples, he breathed that peace on them (John 20-23). We, the modern believers, may use the instructions of Matthew chapter ten to inform us how to work within this peace.

Jesus told his pairs of disciples to go into the towns and villages and seek a worthy person. They are to stay there while serving in that place (Matthew 10:11 – 12). The person will provide for the needs of the disciple. The disciples' gift to the homeowner is the peace of God, not as this world gives peace. The disciples are operating under the authority of Jesus Christ when they loose the peace that is in Heavenly Realms into the Cosmos of the house they are occupying. A worthy person is someone who upholds God's righteousness. Micah 6:8 summarizes God's requirements for righteousness.

He has shown you, O man, what is good; and what does the LORD require of you? But to do justly, to love mercy, and to walk humbly with your God?

The homeowner is to be humble before God and humanity. They are to demonstrate mercy and act justly to neighbors. When the time of serving in that community is over the disciple was to choose to leave the peace or take back the blessing (Matthew10:13).

In modern times, we have the Holy Spirit to discern whether a provider meets the requirements of Micah 6:8. This is why the living spiritual love is to be embedded in the hearts of Jesus' followers. Believers are also reminded to examine themselves first before someone else (Matthew 7:3 – 5). We are given the Holy Spirit who discerns our hearts and convicts us of anything not in the will of God (1 John 3:19 – 21 & John 16:8). It is only from a place of humility and close intimate relationship with God a believer may discern this truth. Prayer is the key to knowing how a disciple is to leave the community one has served (1 John 5:14). If a disciple is rejected from serving in a community, the person is to simply dust the feet off and move on. Under the authority of Jesus Christ, there is to be no ownership of one's actions. Jesus warned his people would be rejected just as he was (1 John 3:13). These verses emphasize living in humility and dependency on Jesus Christ as one serves in a community.

To operate in the peace that passes understanding requires specific attitudes of the soul-heart. As explained in the last paragraph, the first attitude is humility. This attitude includes a willingness to serve others in love, not judgment. The second attitude is demonstrated in the next verse, Matthew 10:16

> *"Behold, I send you out as sheep in the midst of wolves. Therefore, be wise as serpents and harmless as doves."*

Jesus is recognizing the fallen condition of the governments of the world. Because every person is born with the Tree of Knowledge of Good and Evil within their soul, the governments created by humanity do not reflect the Kingdom of God principles. Believers in Christ Jesus as Lord are now recognized as ambassadors of the Kingdom of God (2 Corinthians 5:20). Our alliance is to the Kingdom of God above any government of humanity. Jesus compares these governments as wolves, seeking to devour and destroy his ambassadors. Functioning from humility and demonstrating the love of God is interpreted by the worldview standards as weak, like sheep (1 Corinthians 2:14). Yet we have the authority and power of the one who has overcome the devil and all his power and works (Luke 10:19). We are to be wise in the ways of the world that functions within the Tree of knowledge of Good and Evil yet not subject ourselves to it. In other words, know in the soul-mind how we had thought and behaved before accepting Jesus Christ as Lord. Since our authority and power is from God, and not of ourselves, we can still function in love and humility. We can trust God and his ways in all things knowing God will lead us.

A further warning is given by Jesus to his disciples (Matthew 10:17 – 19).

Expect to be brought before representatives of these governments for acting under the authority of Jesus Christ. Jesus promises when this happens, God

will be with them. Disciples are warned to stand in faith not fear. As recorded in Matthew 10:19 - 20

> *[19]"But when they deliver you up, do not worry about how or what you should speak. For it will be given to you in that hour what you should speak; [20]for it is not you who speak, but the Spirit of your Father who speaks in you."*

The attitude of the soul-heart recommended in these passages is one of trust in God not one's own understanding. It is living Proverbs 3:5 -6. Like the attitudes of humility, loving others and not judging others, this attitude is practiced and learned while applying scriptures daily to one's life.

John, the disciple who called himself the beloved of God, sums up the attitude of heart we need to embrace to walk in this living spiritual love. As he wrote in 1John 4:10 – 12

> *[10]In this is love, not that we loved God, but that He loved us and sent His Son to be the propitiation for our sins. [11]Beloved, if God so loved us, we also ought to love one another. [12]No one has seen God at any time. If we love one another, God abides in us, and His love has been perfected in us.*

Our gift of love at the altar of God is to love others as God has loved us. Only by receiving and knowing this living spiritual love can we love others in this manner. It requires daily intimate time with our God to maintain this living love. Jesus stands at the door of your heart and is knocking asking if he may come in deeper and bring you into this intimate presence of God (Revelations 3:20)

References

Thomas Nelson: NKJV. Holy Bible. Thomas Nelson. Kindle Edition

Thomas Nelson: NIV. Holy Bible. Thomas Nelson. Kindle Edition

Vine, W. E. Vines, Unger, Merrill, & White Jr. William. Complete Repository Dictionary. (Thomas Nelson Publishers) 1996.

Diane M. Neumann

Additional Books by Author

Available on Amazon

Weapons of Praise. 2020

The Power of Discipleship. 2020

Seeking God's Righteousness. 2021

Covenant: A Relationship Between Two Kingdoms. 2021

Grace: An Attribute of God. 2022

God's Resting Place. 2022

Breaking Chains Through the Power of Christ Jesus. 2021

Prophetic Battle Plan: Praying God's Kingdom Principles into Our World. 2022

*A*dvantage
BOOKS

advbookstore.com
we bring dreams to life ™

Diane M. Neumann